Santorini, Greece
Coloring books for adults

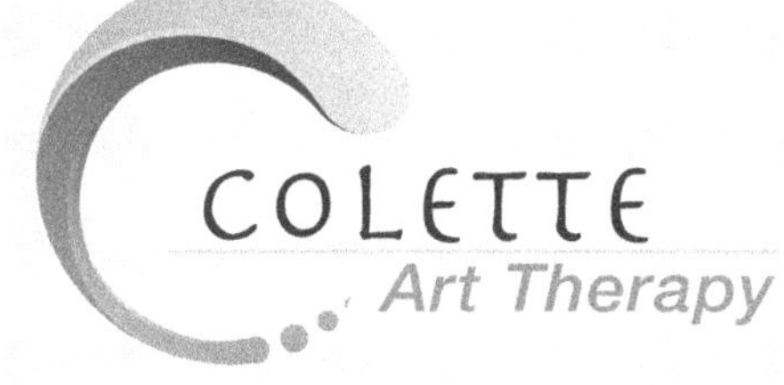

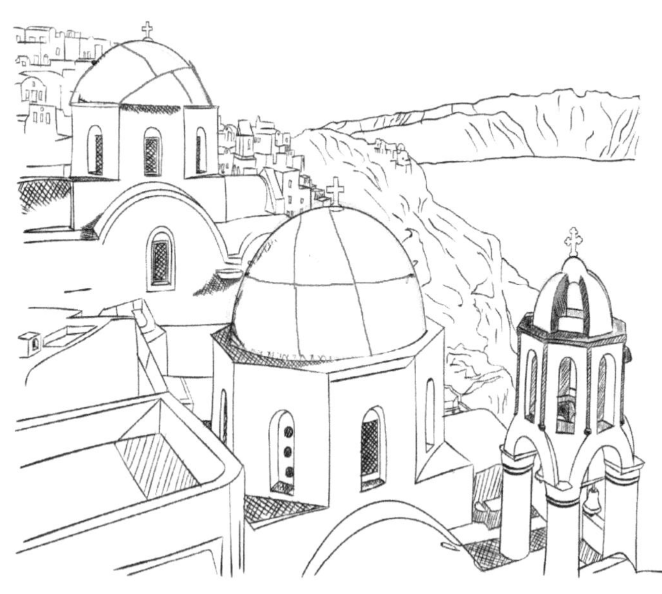

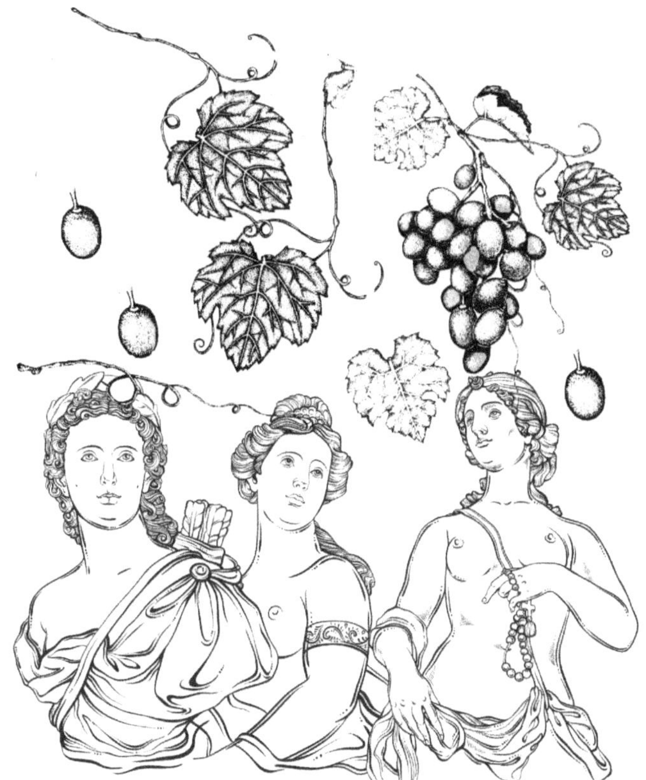

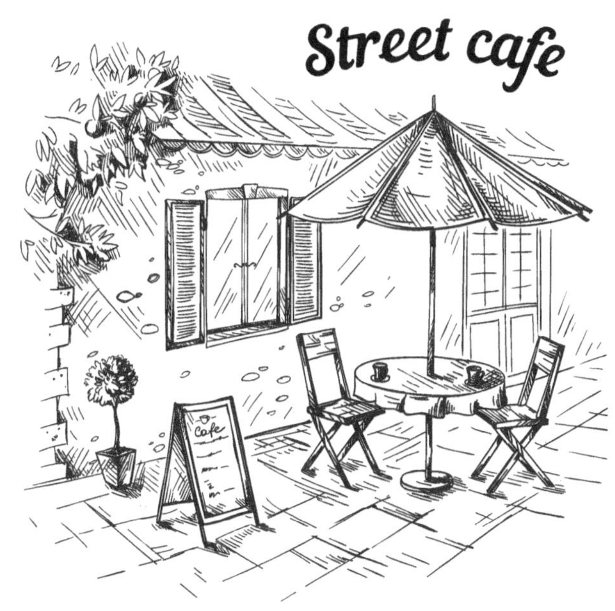

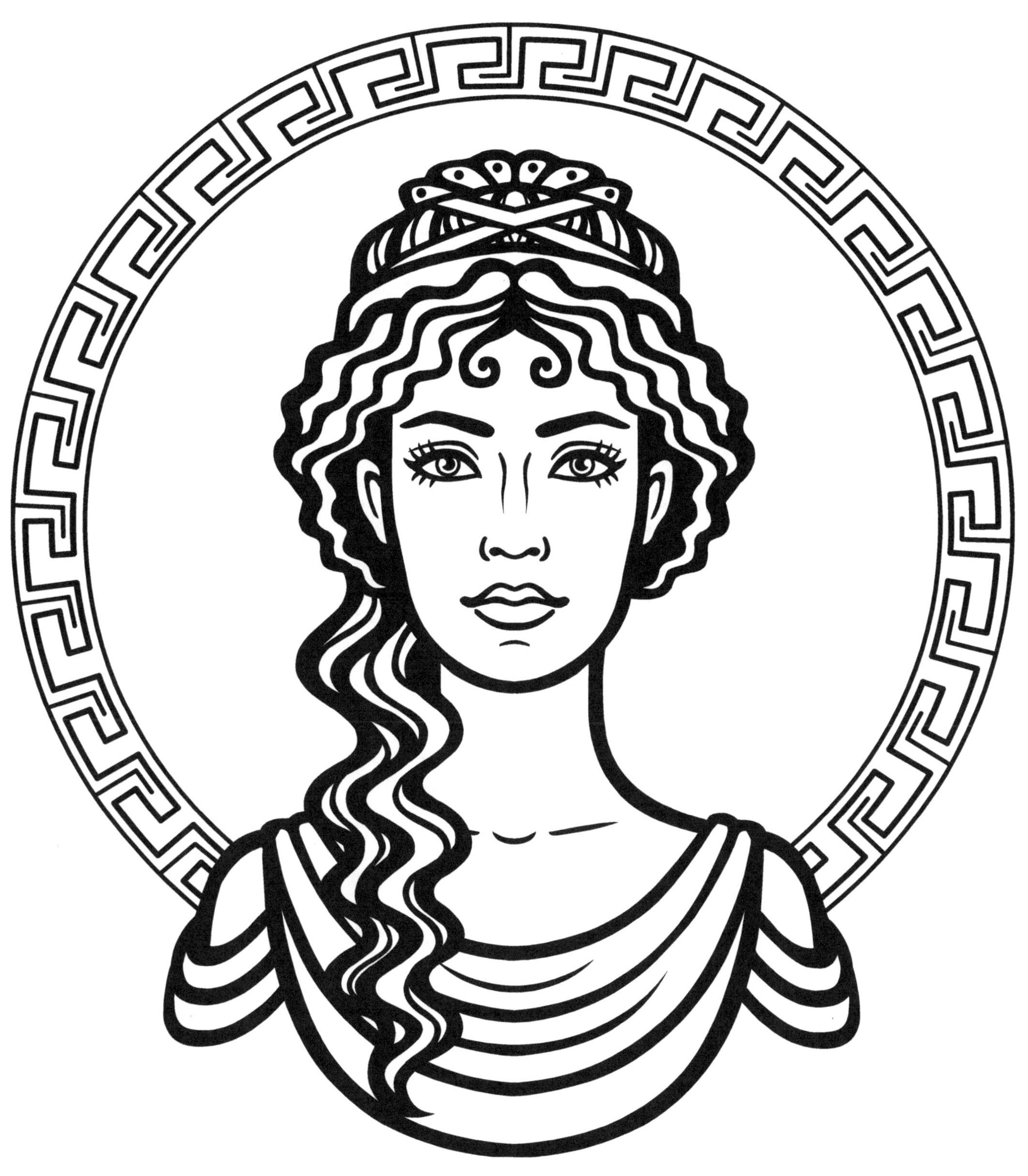

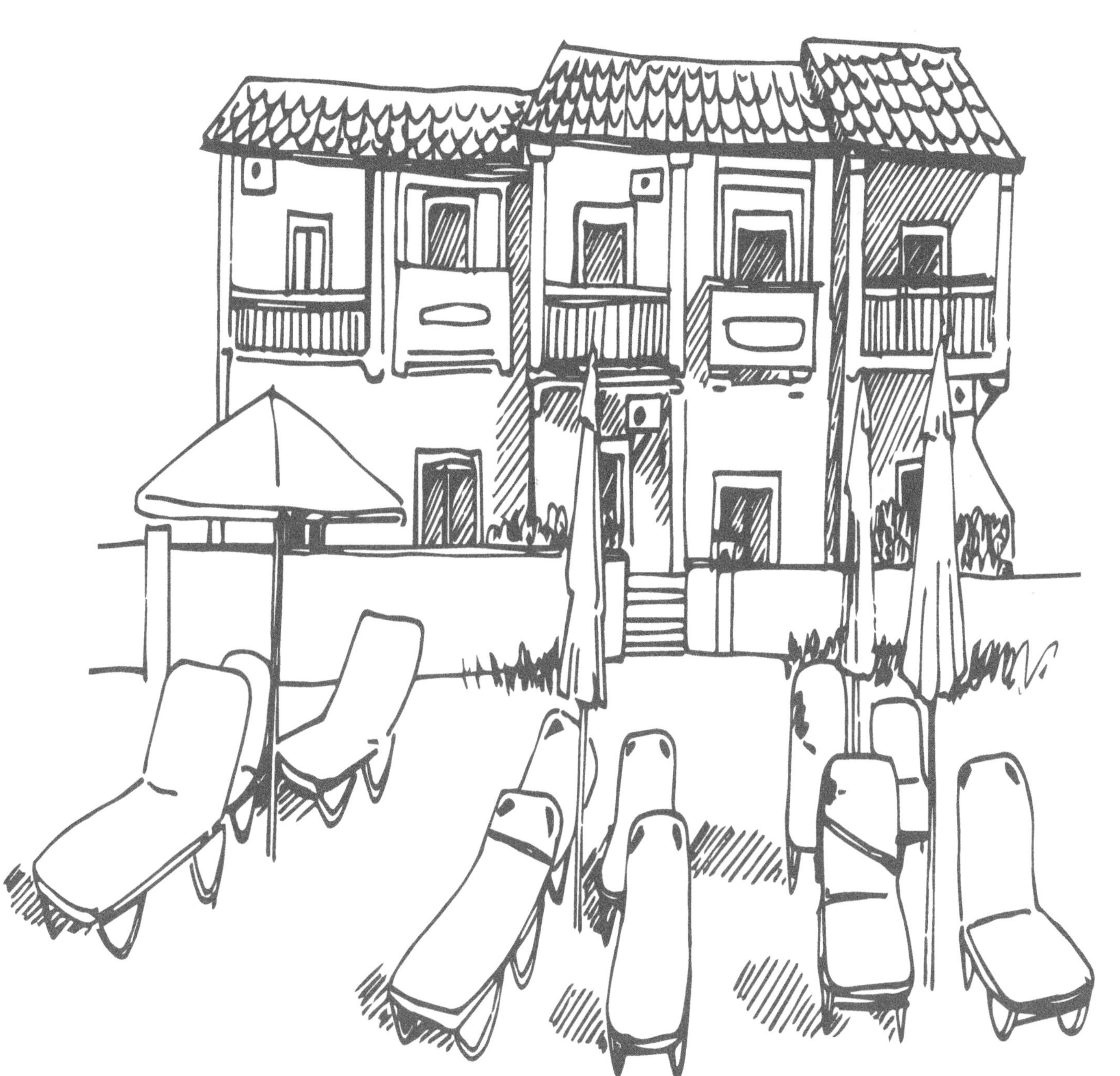

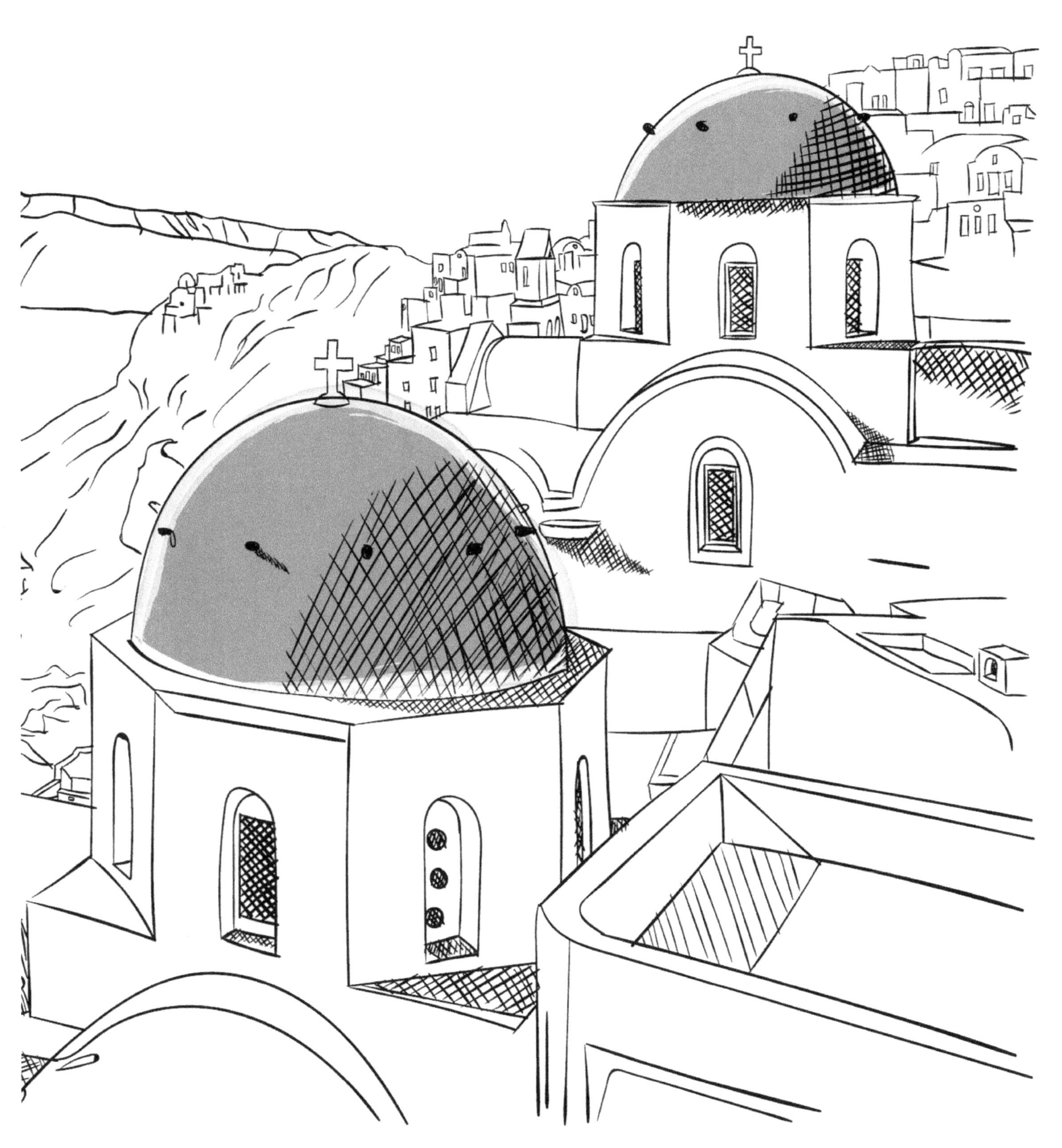

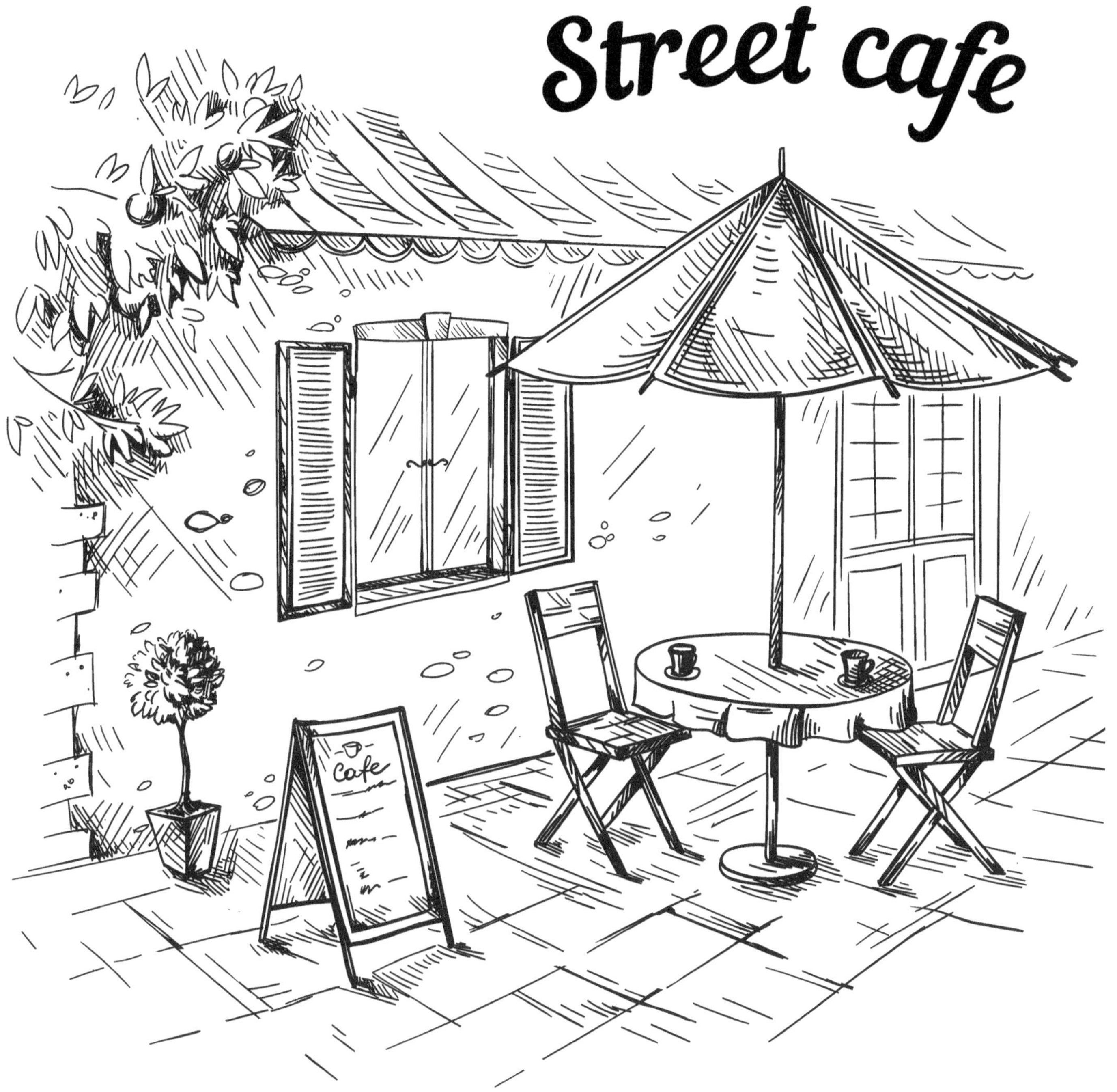

Street cafe
Cafe

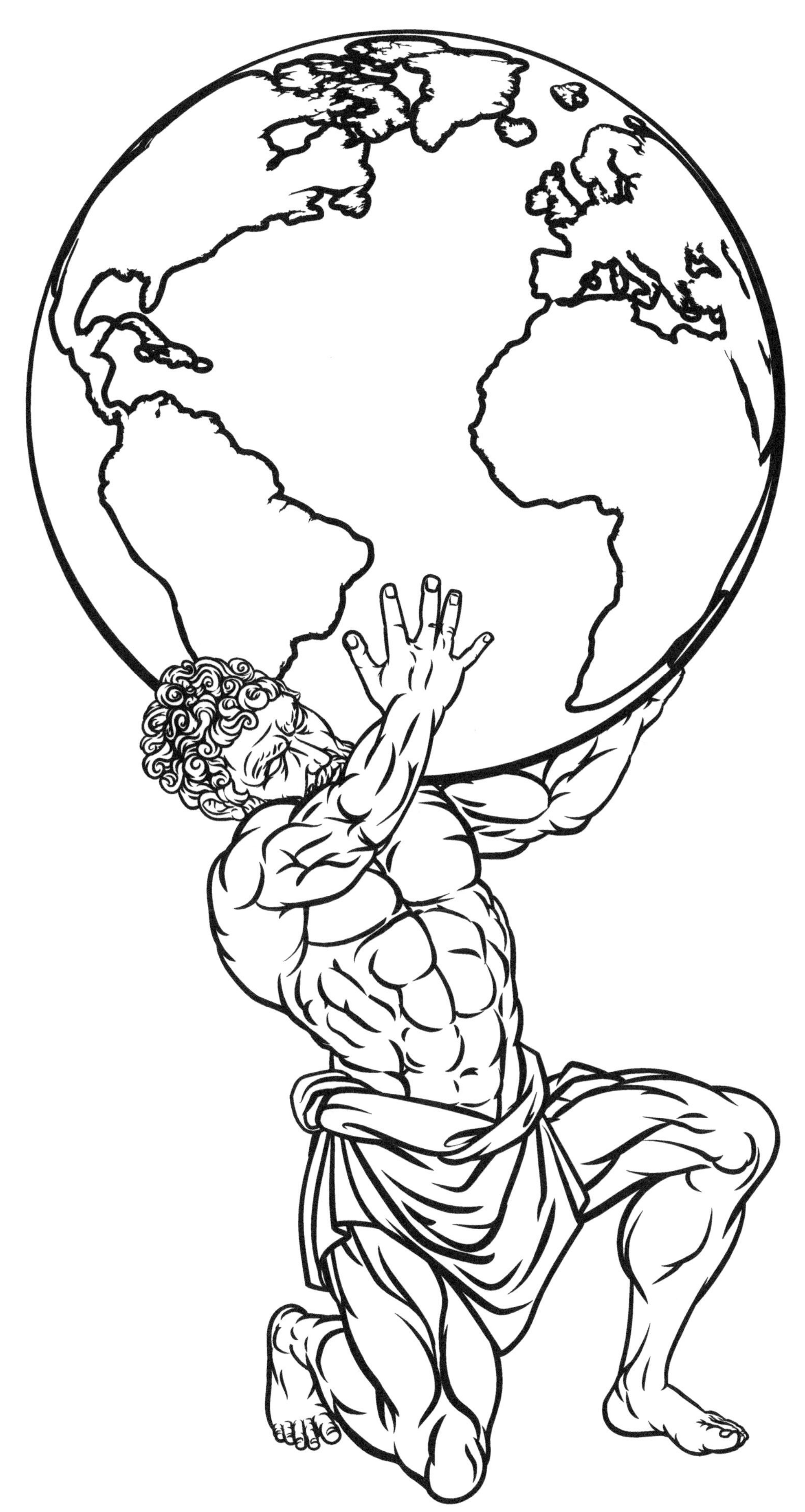

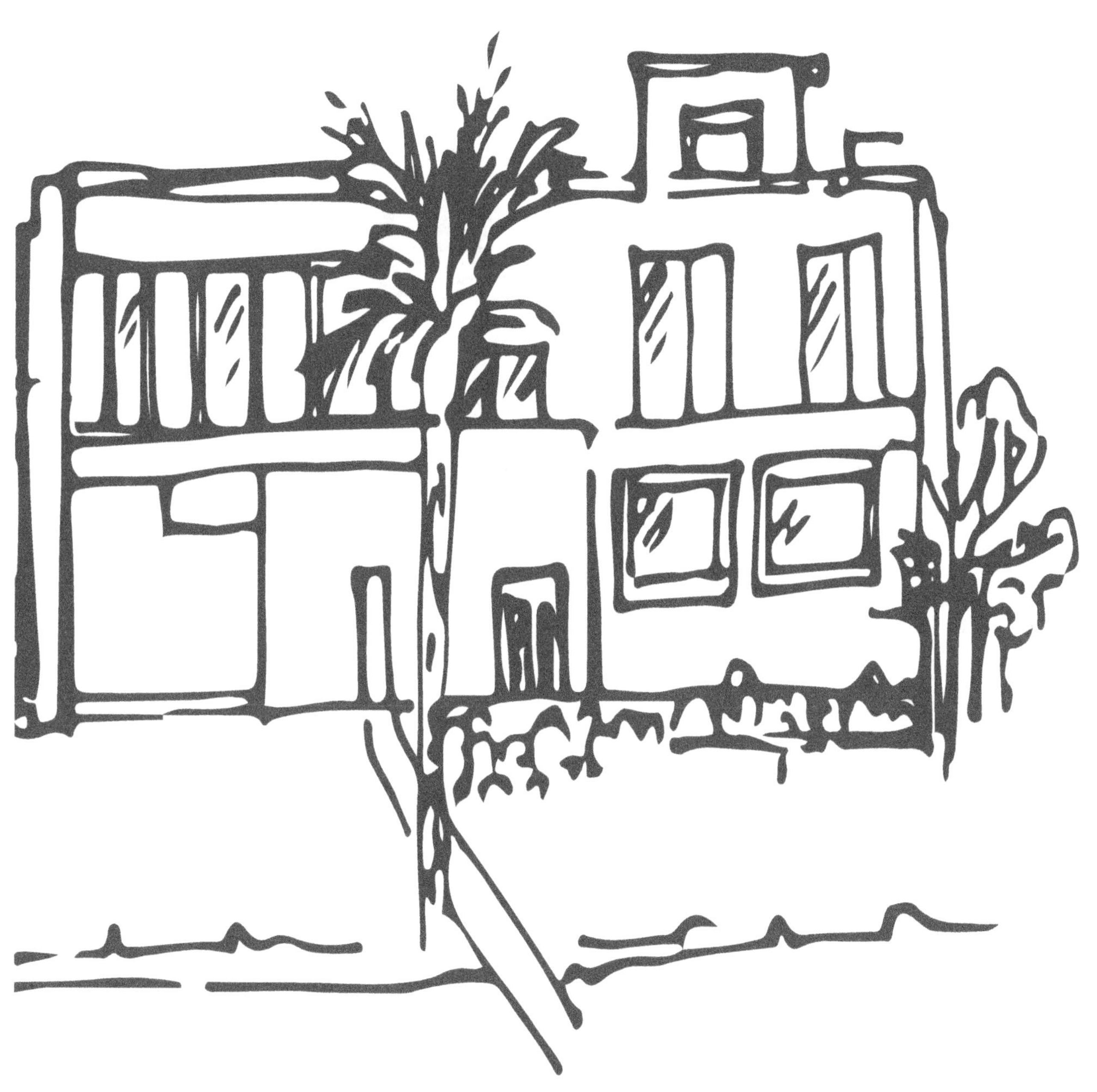

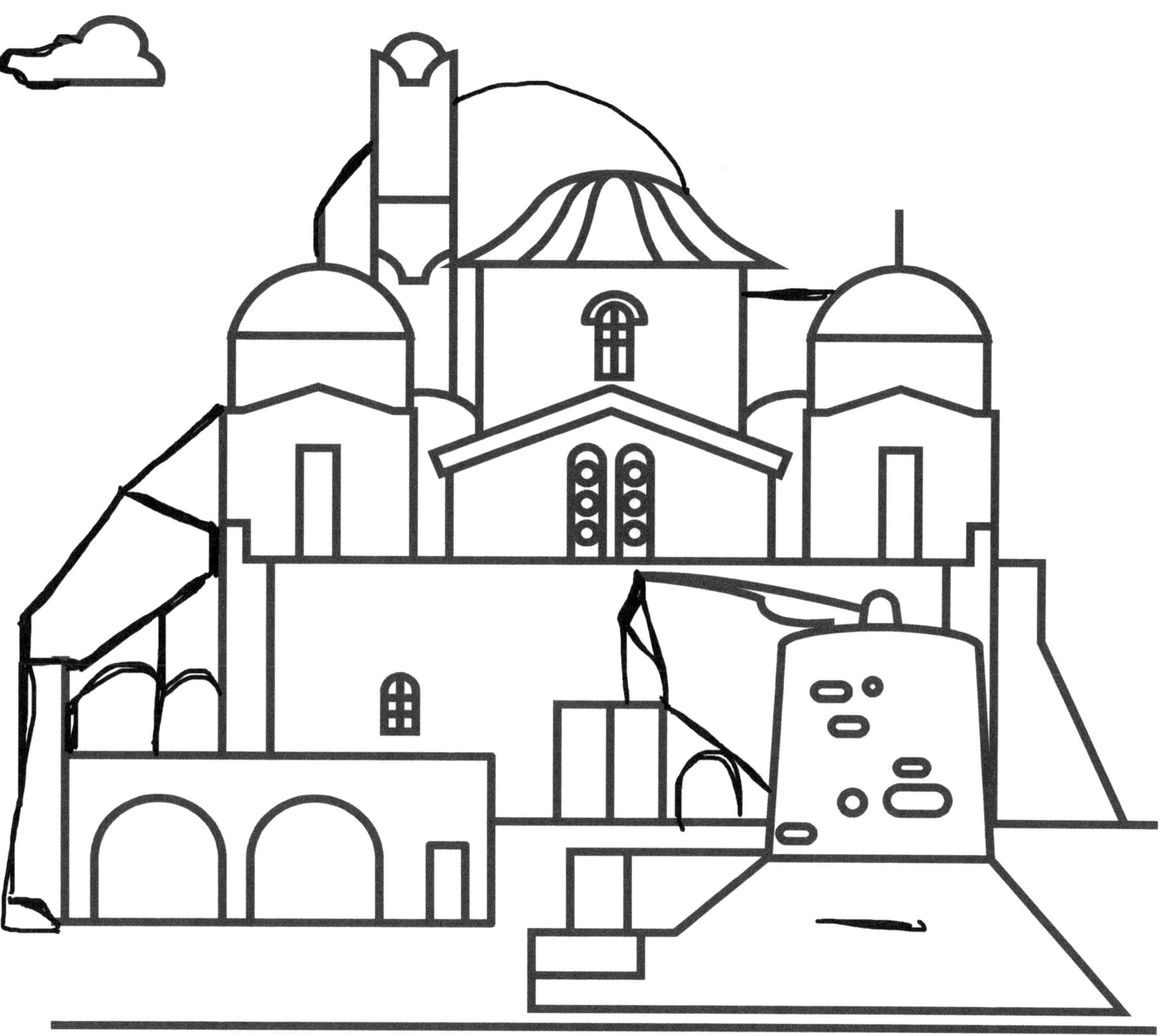

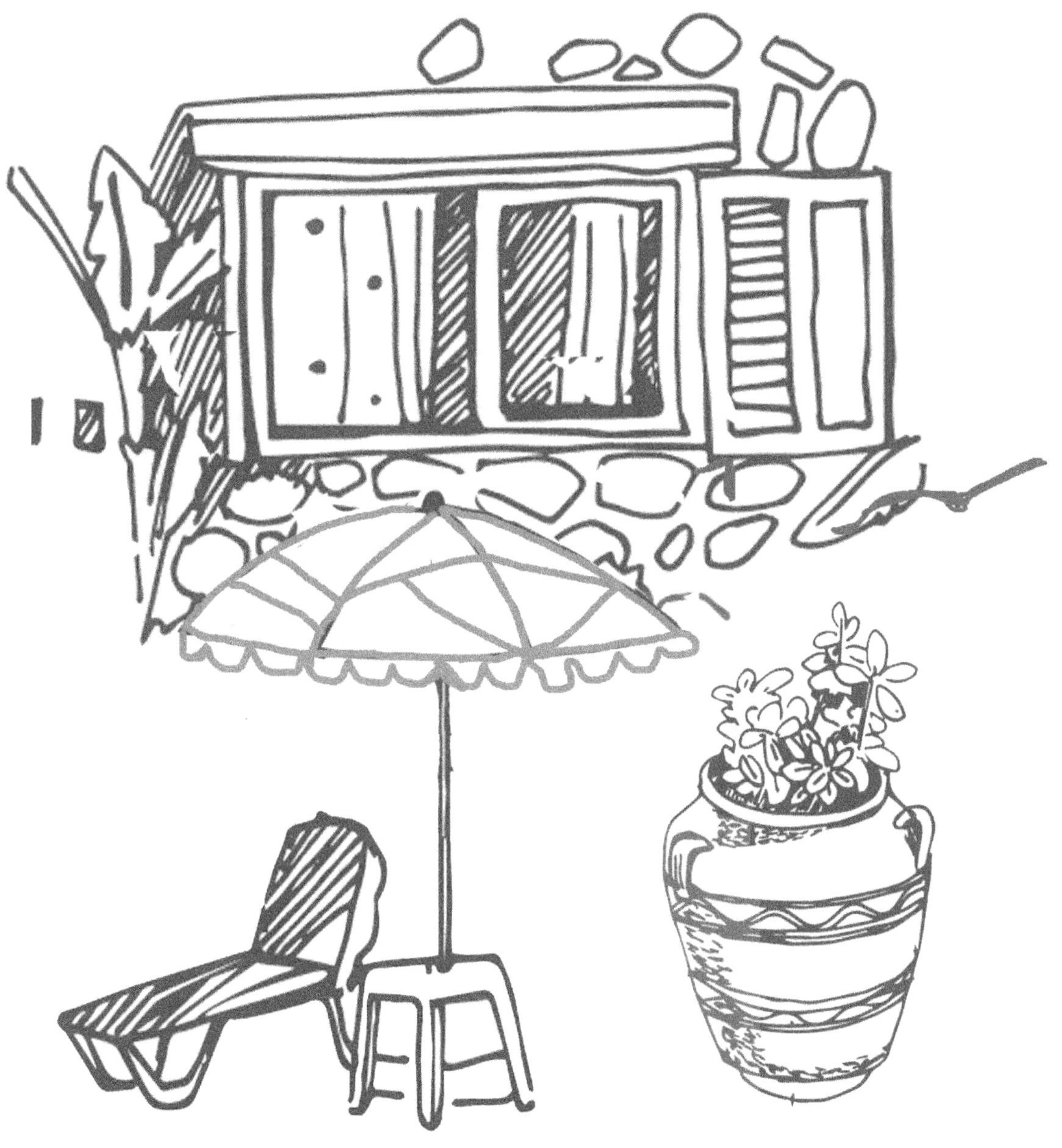

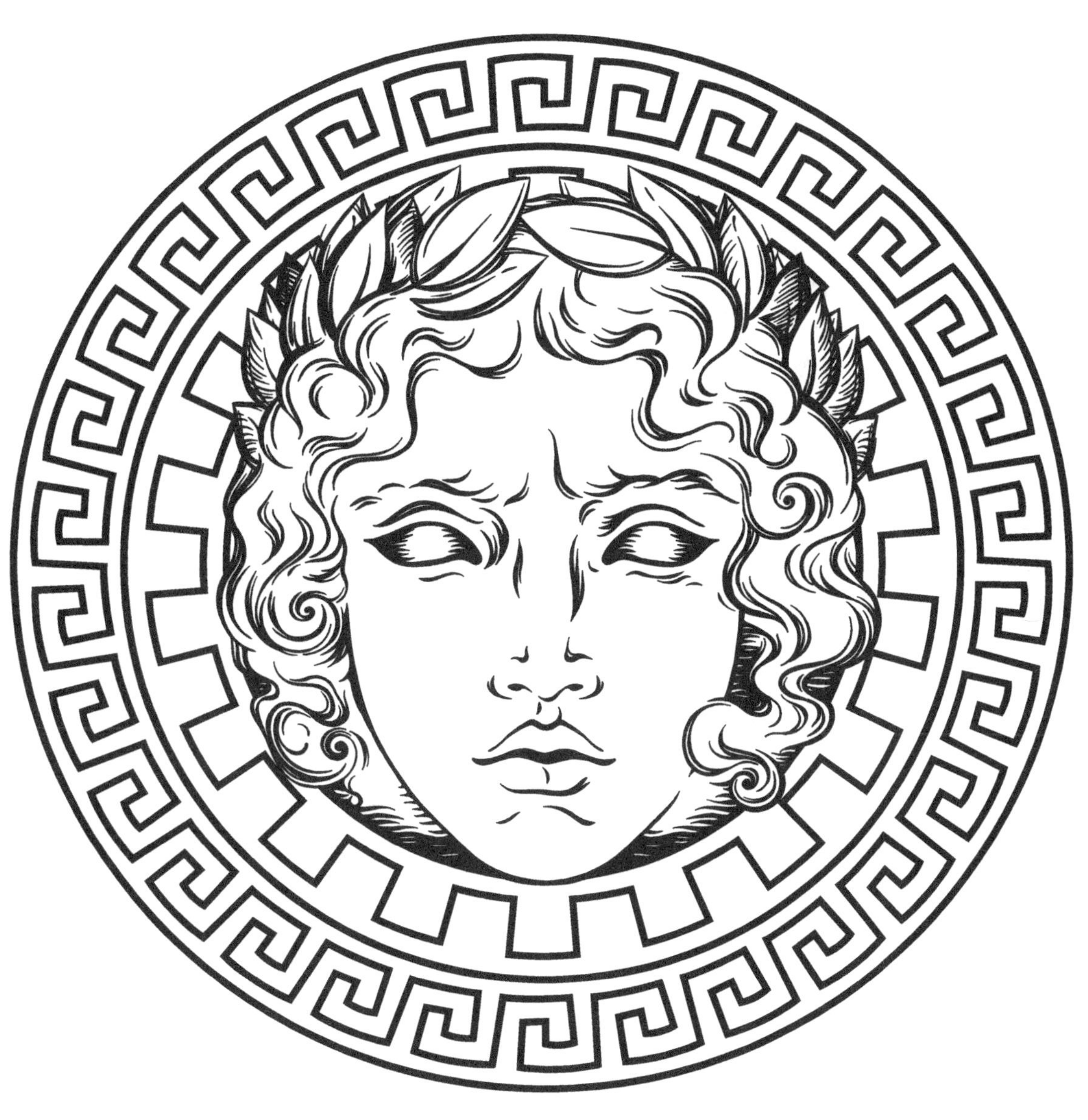

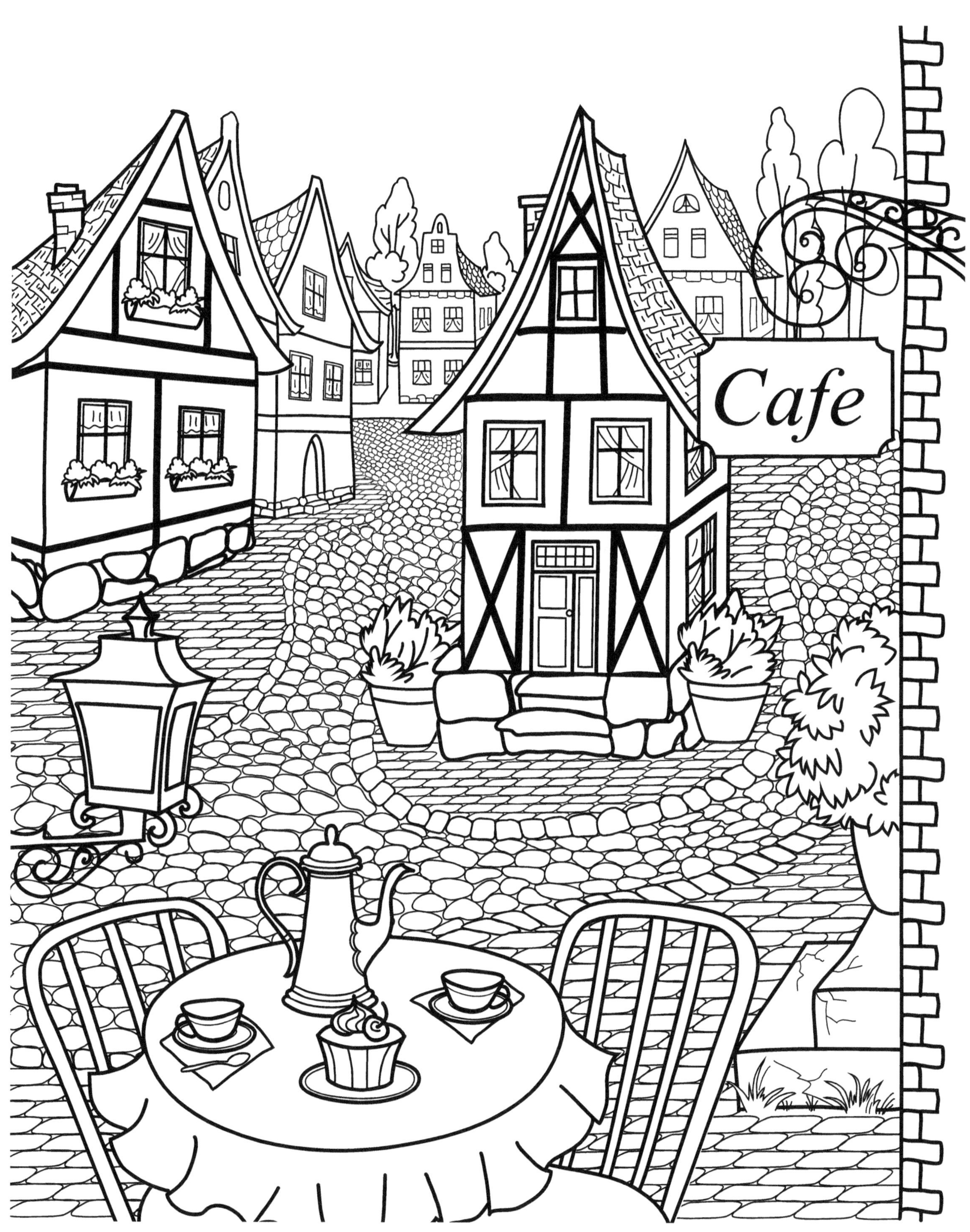
Cafe

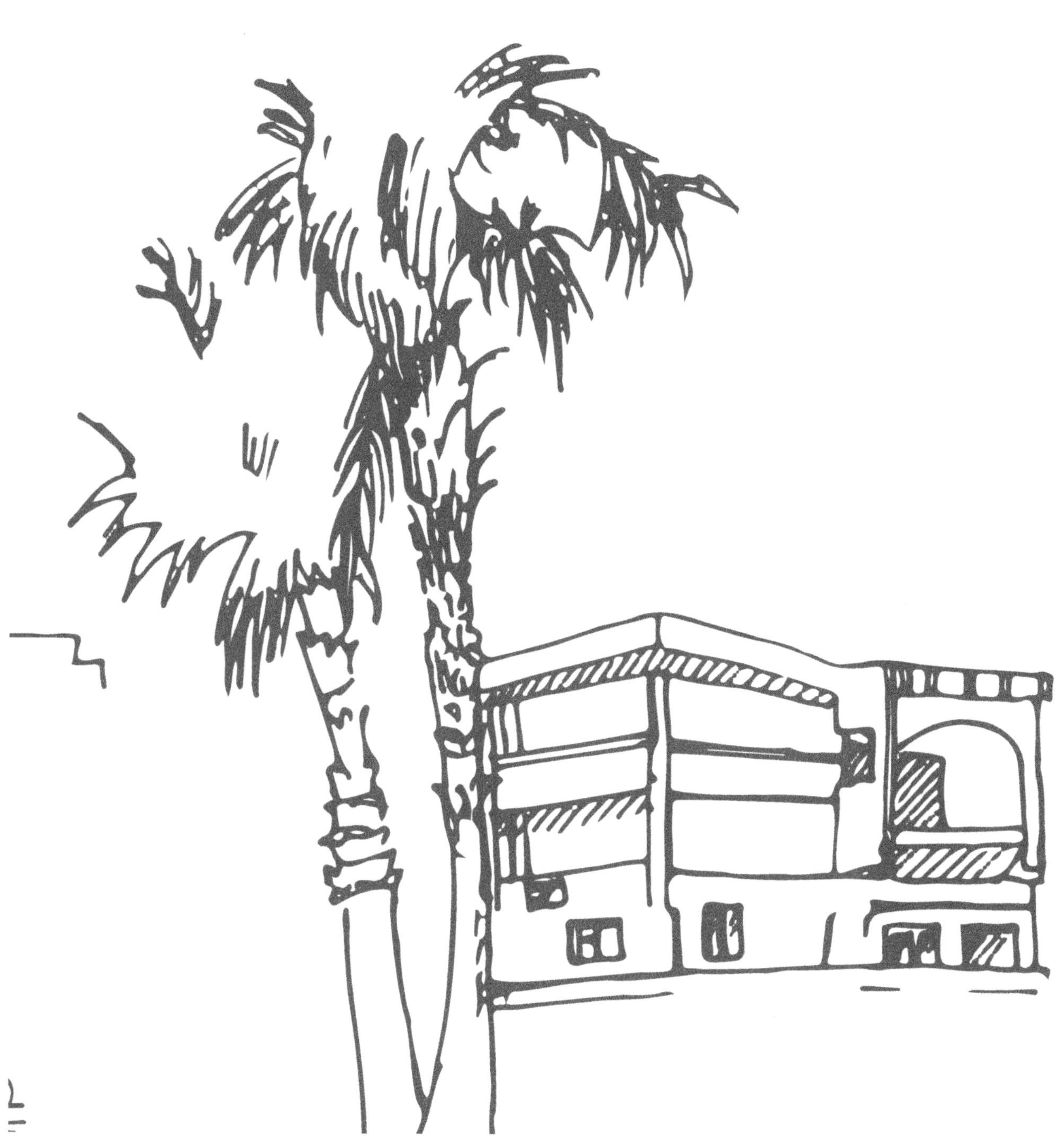

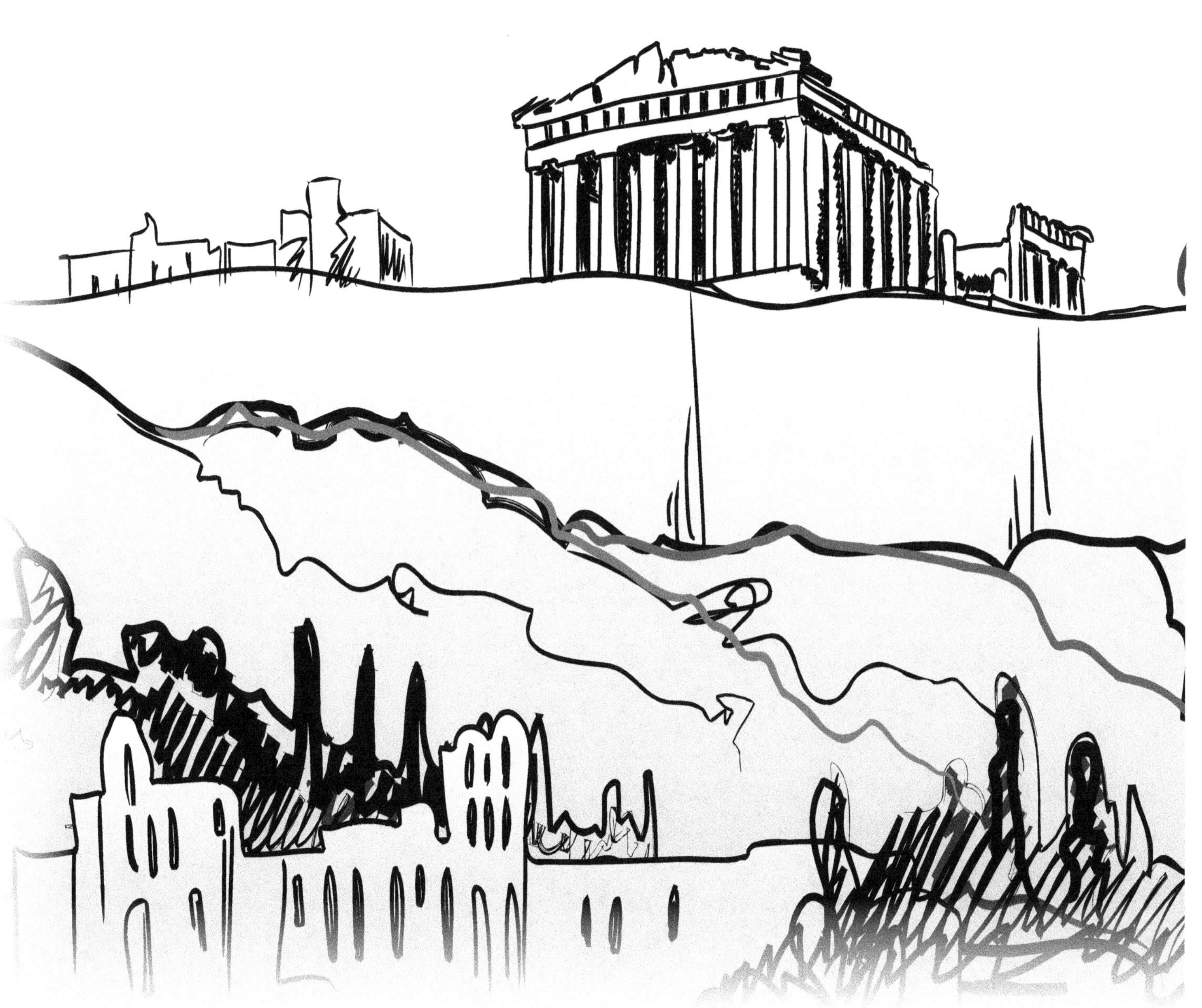

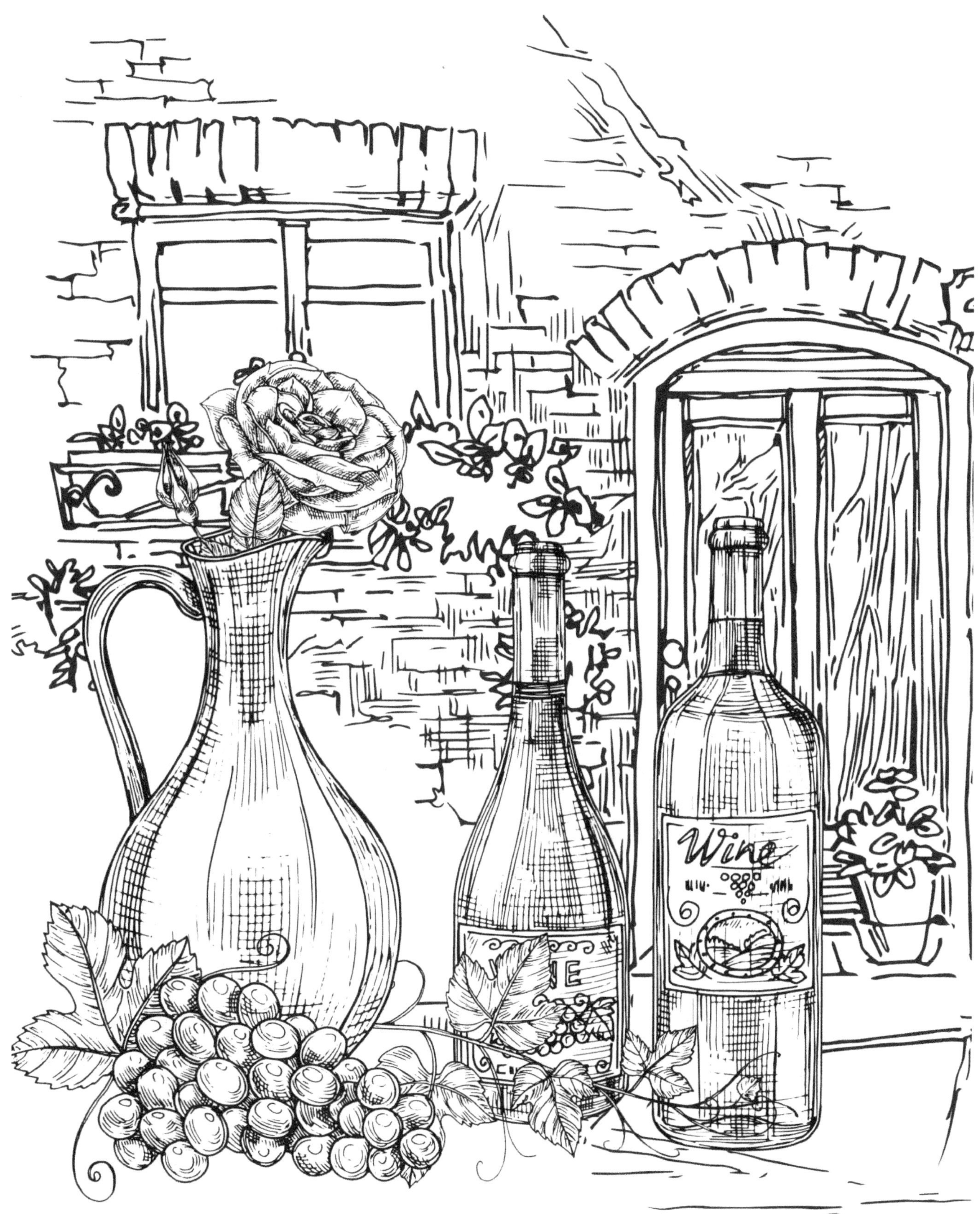

Wine

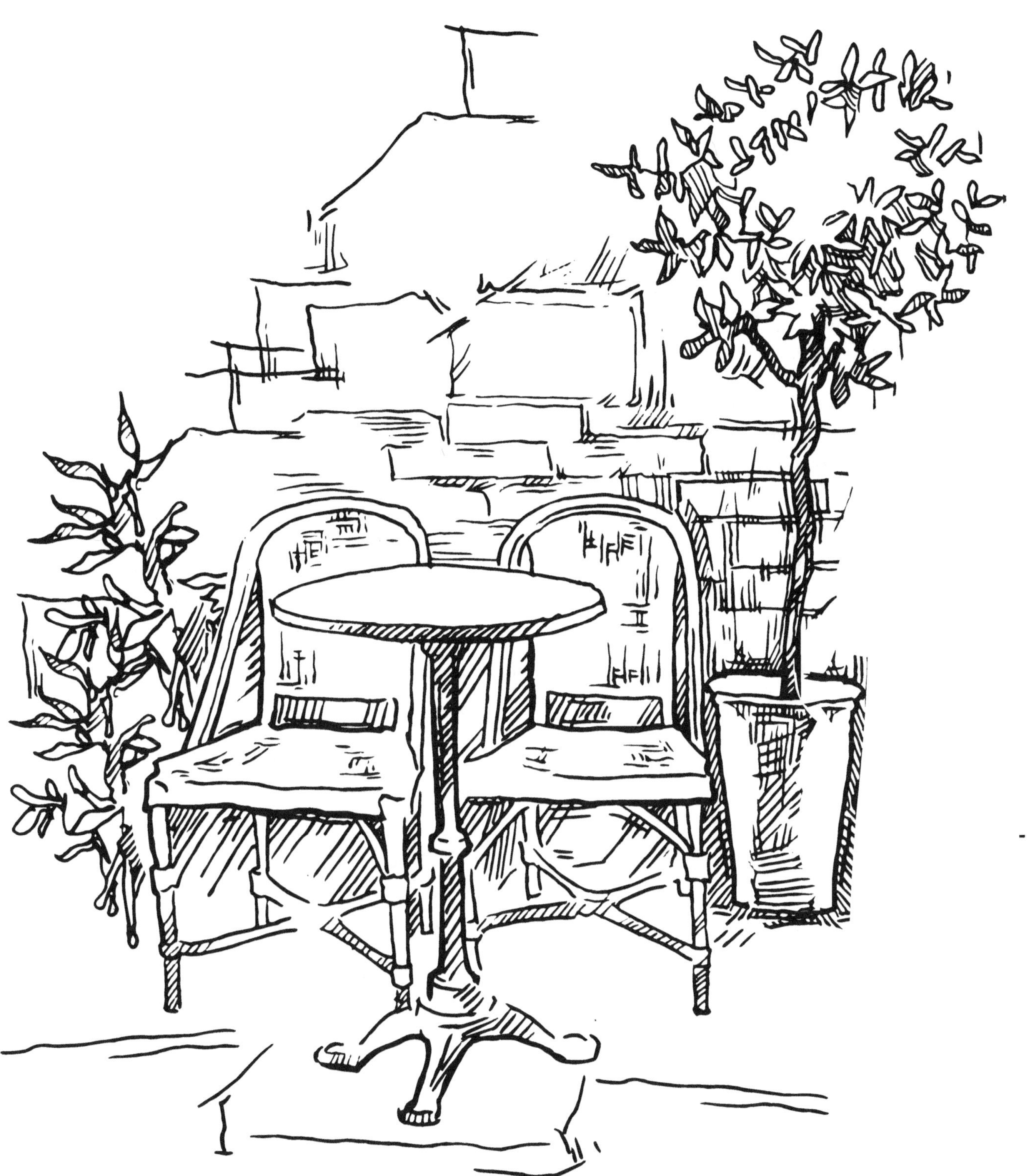

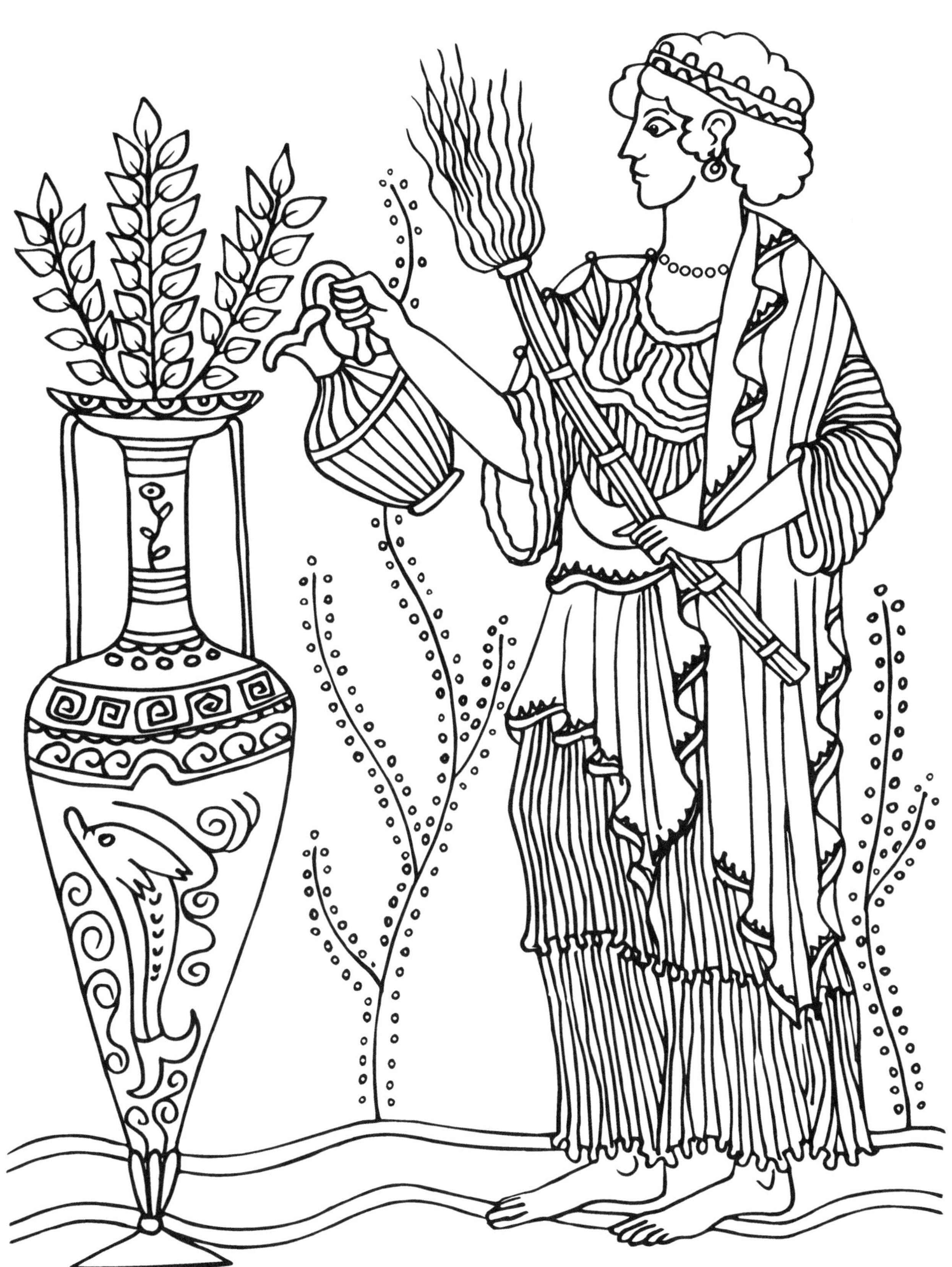

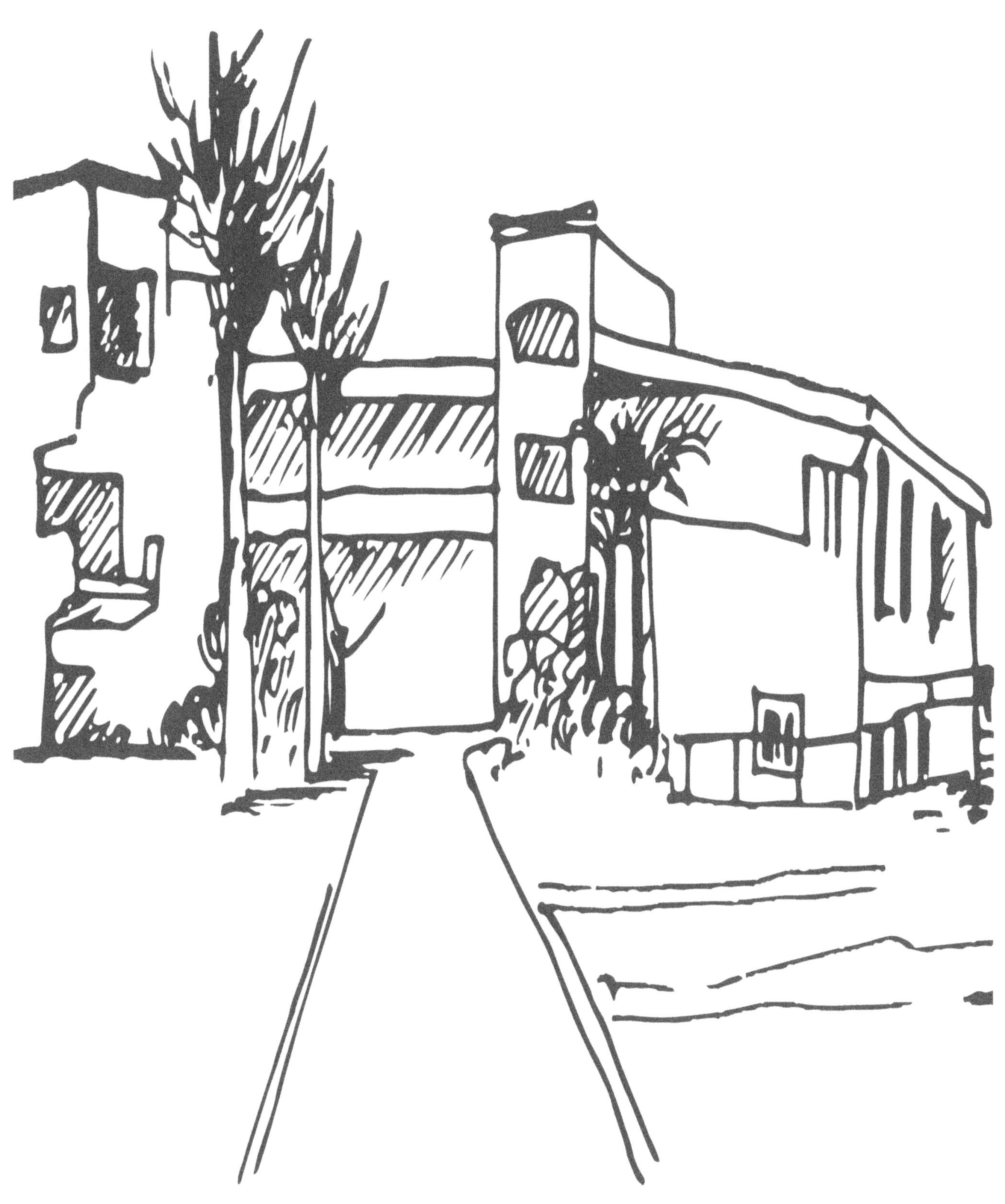

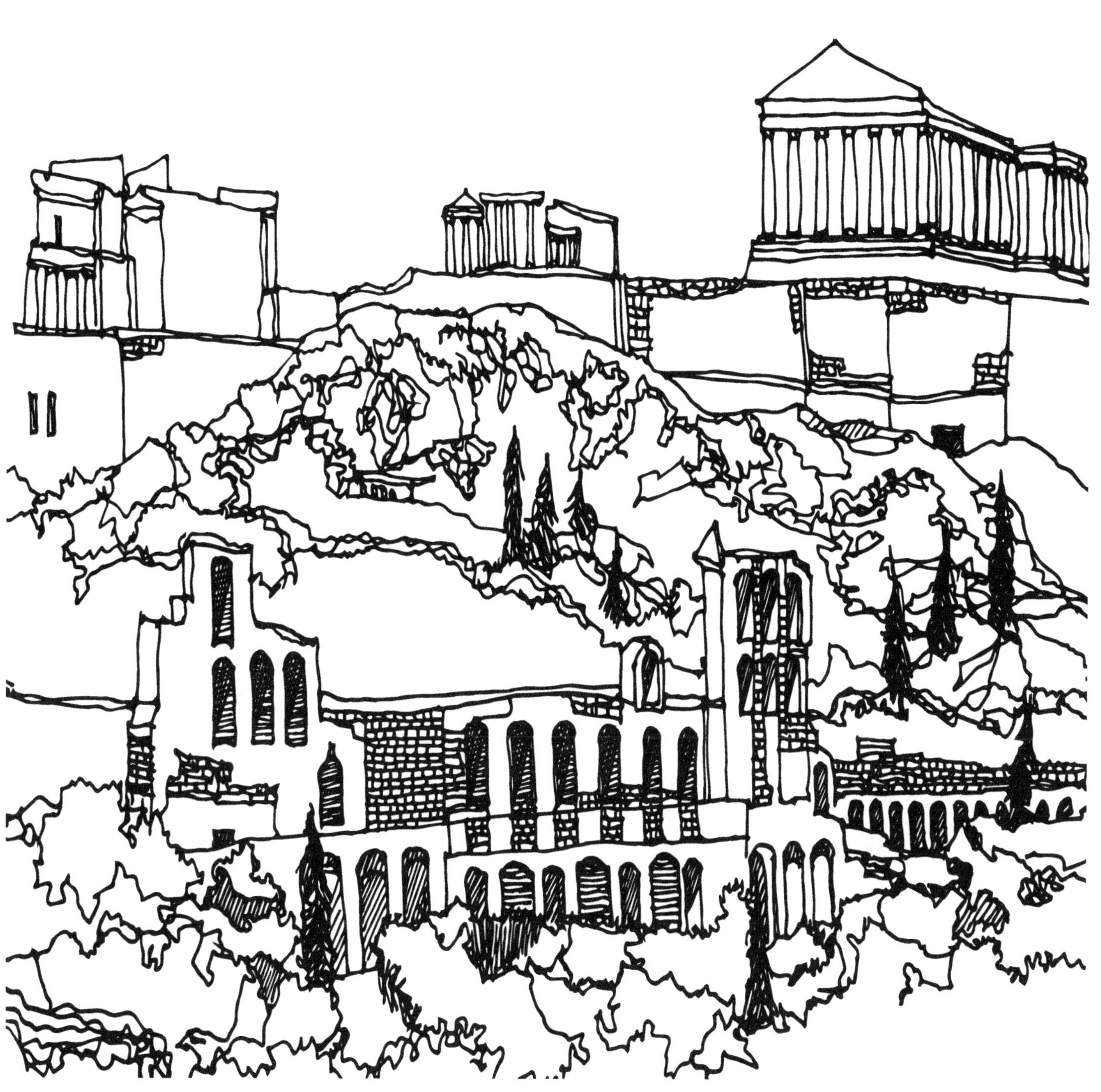

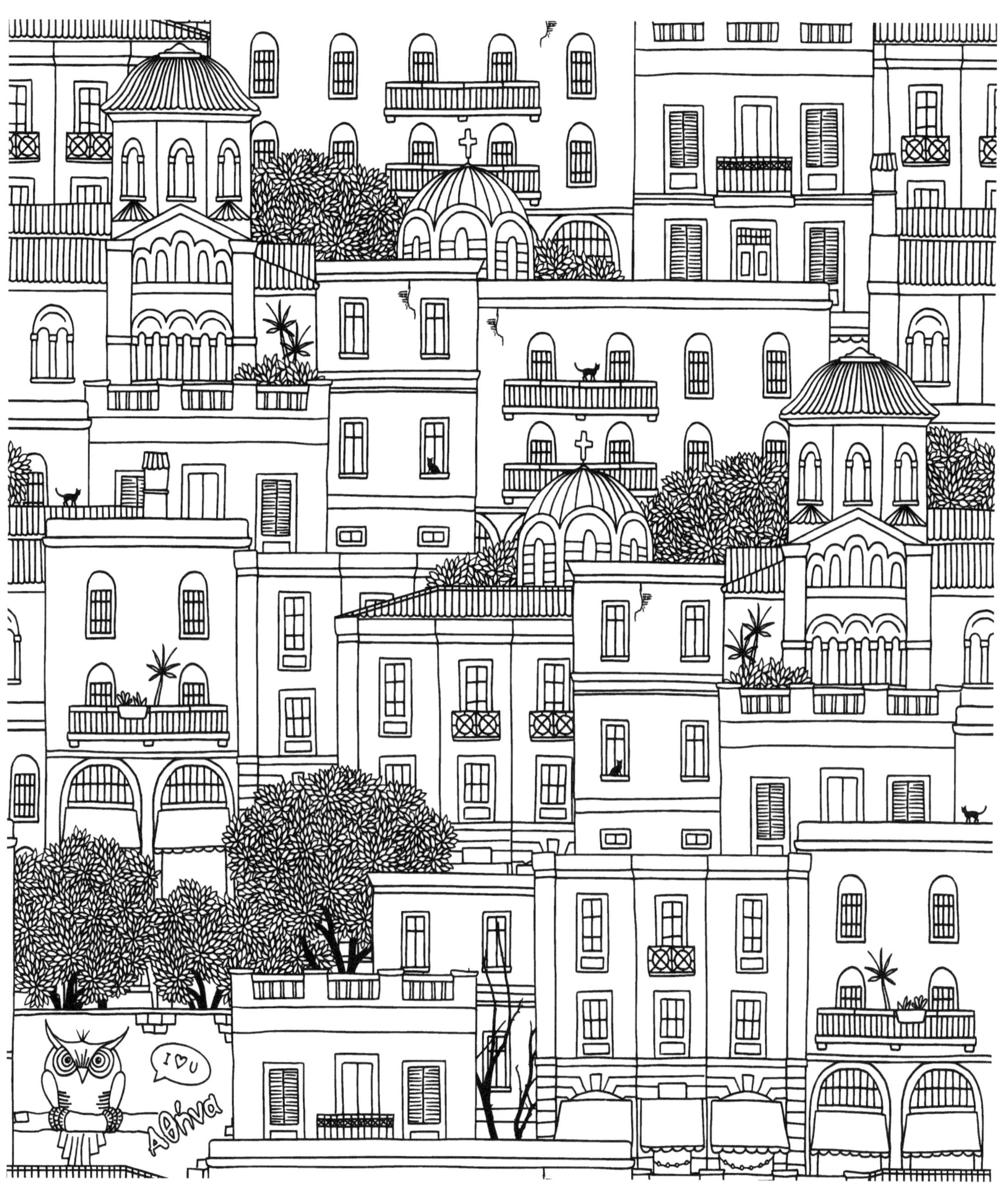

I ♥ U
Αθήνα

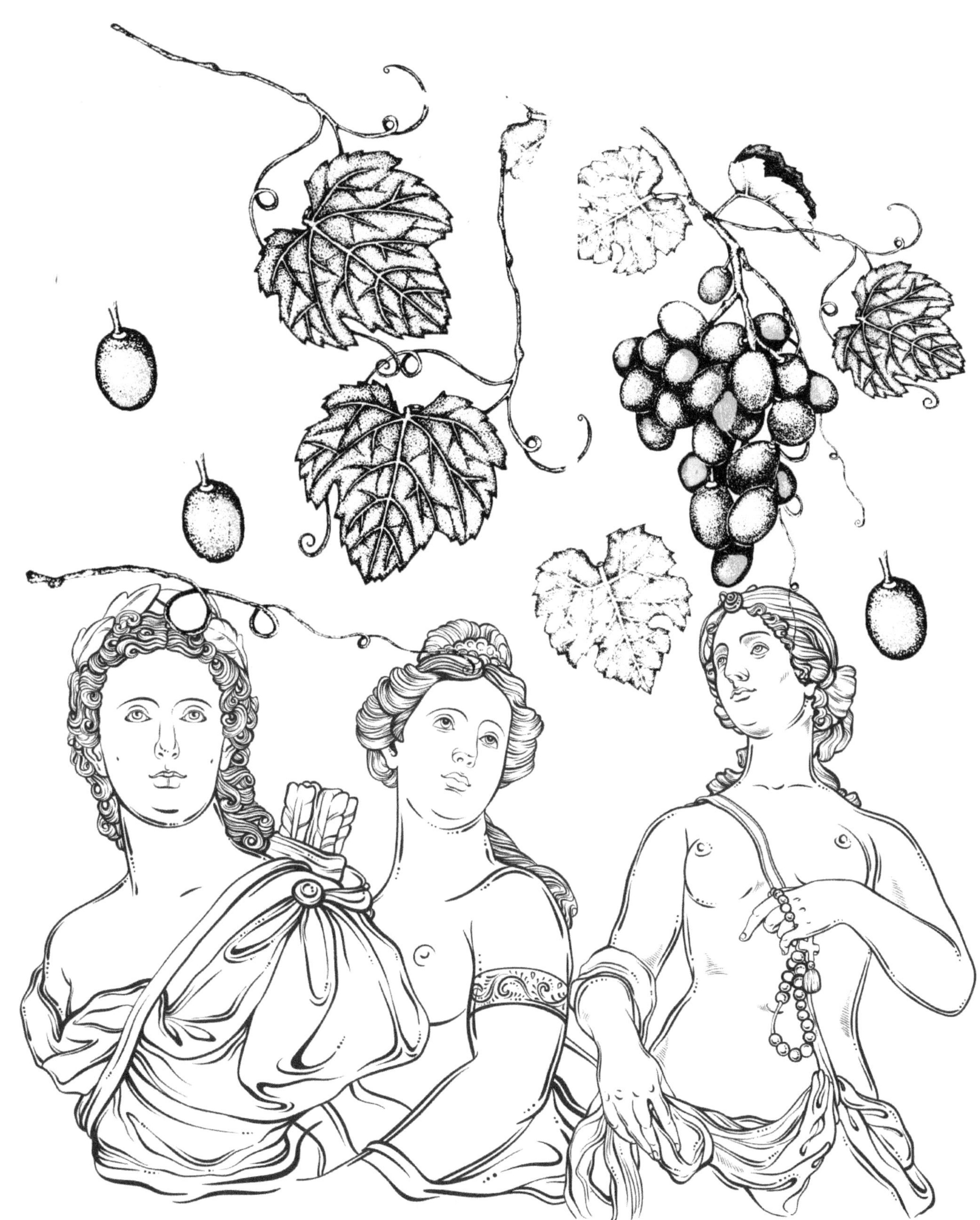

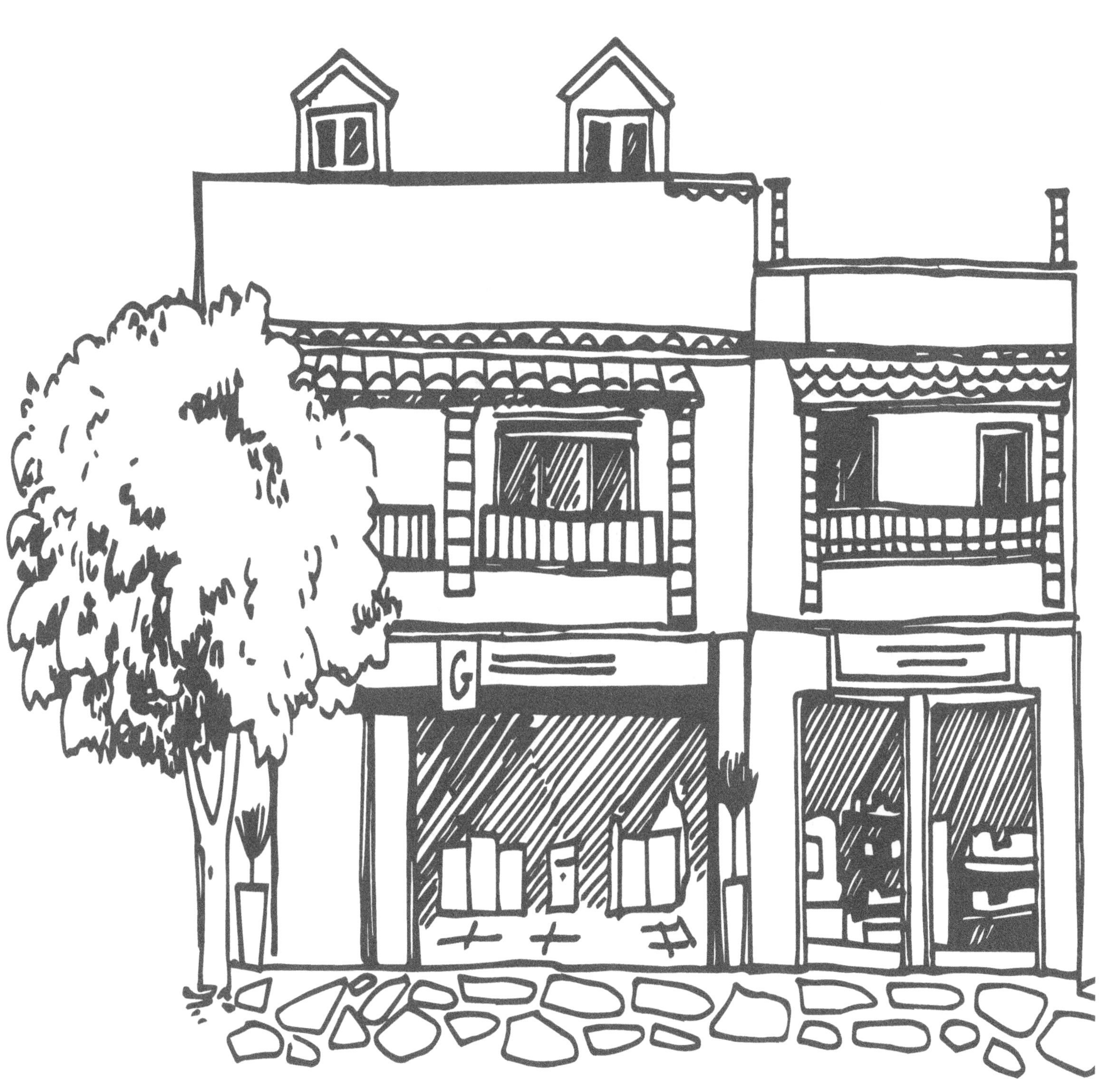

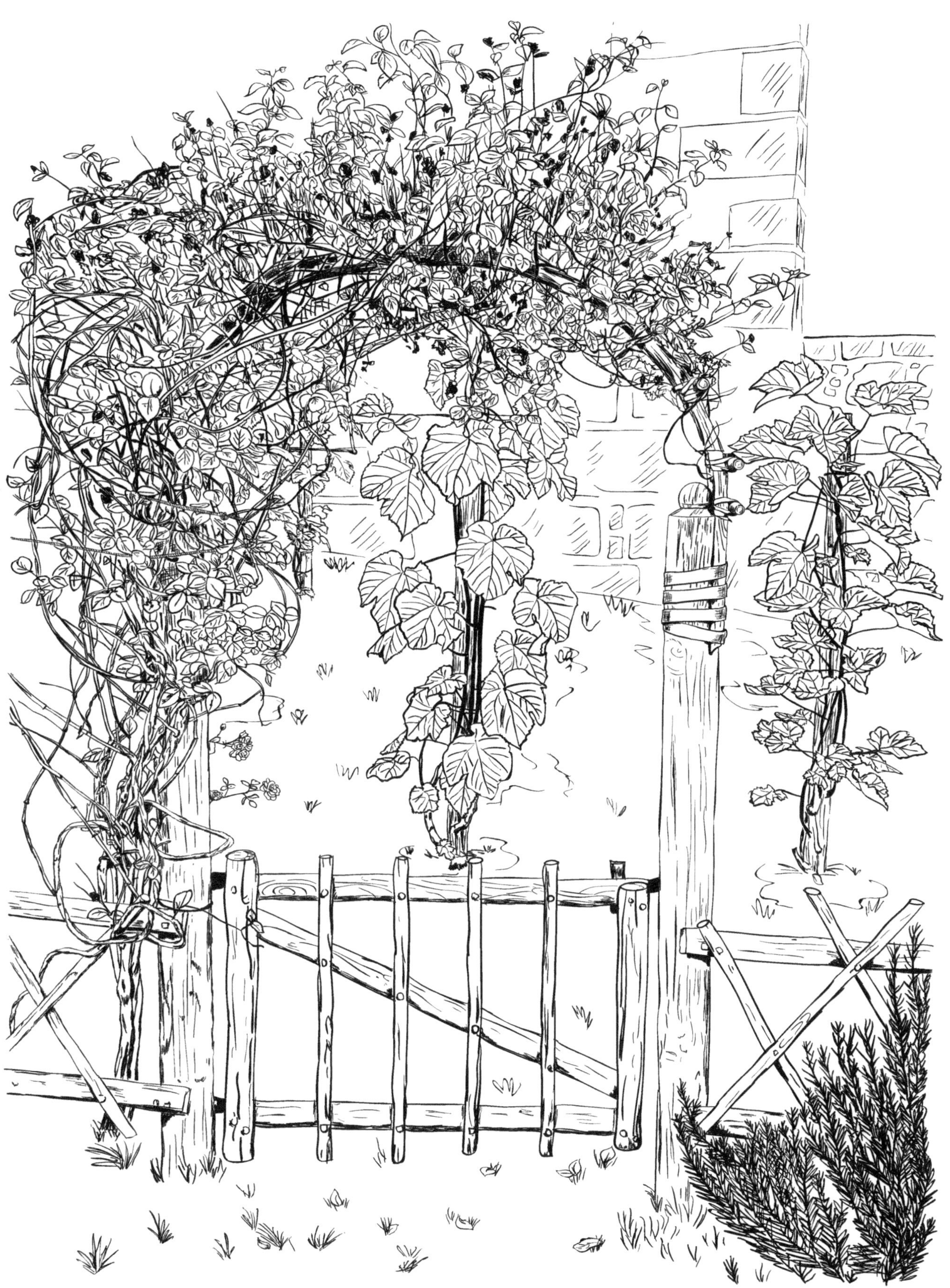

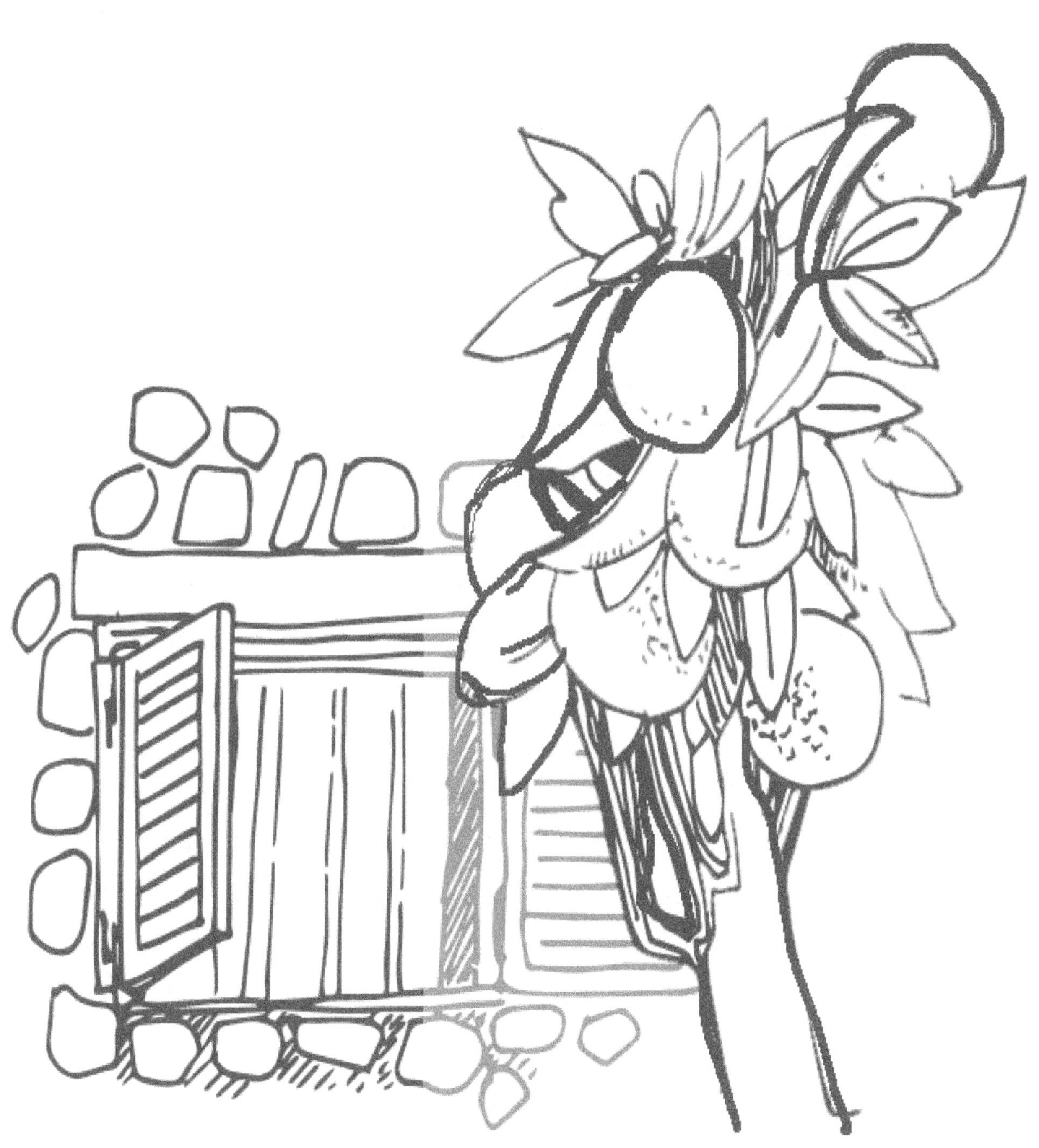

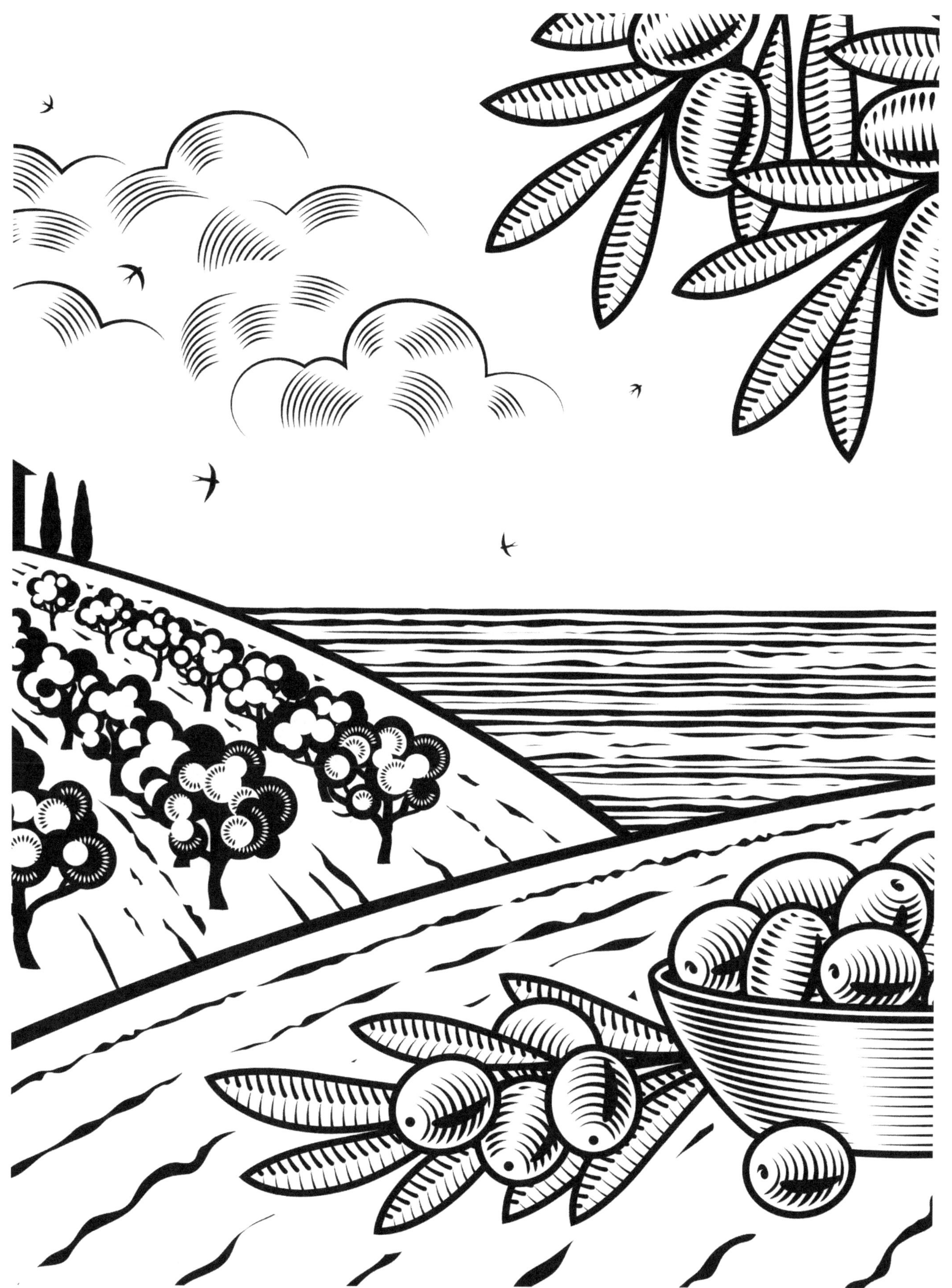

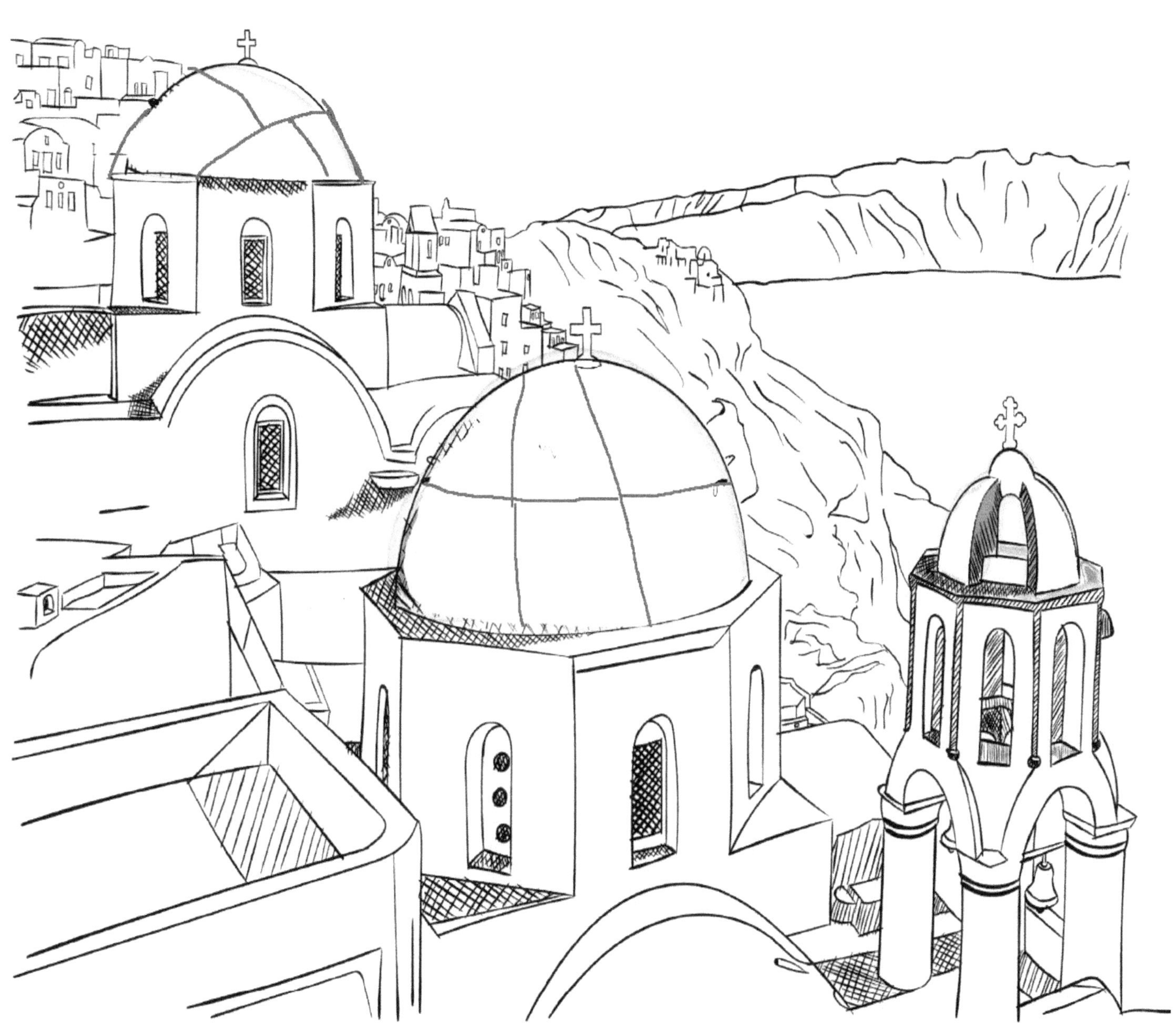

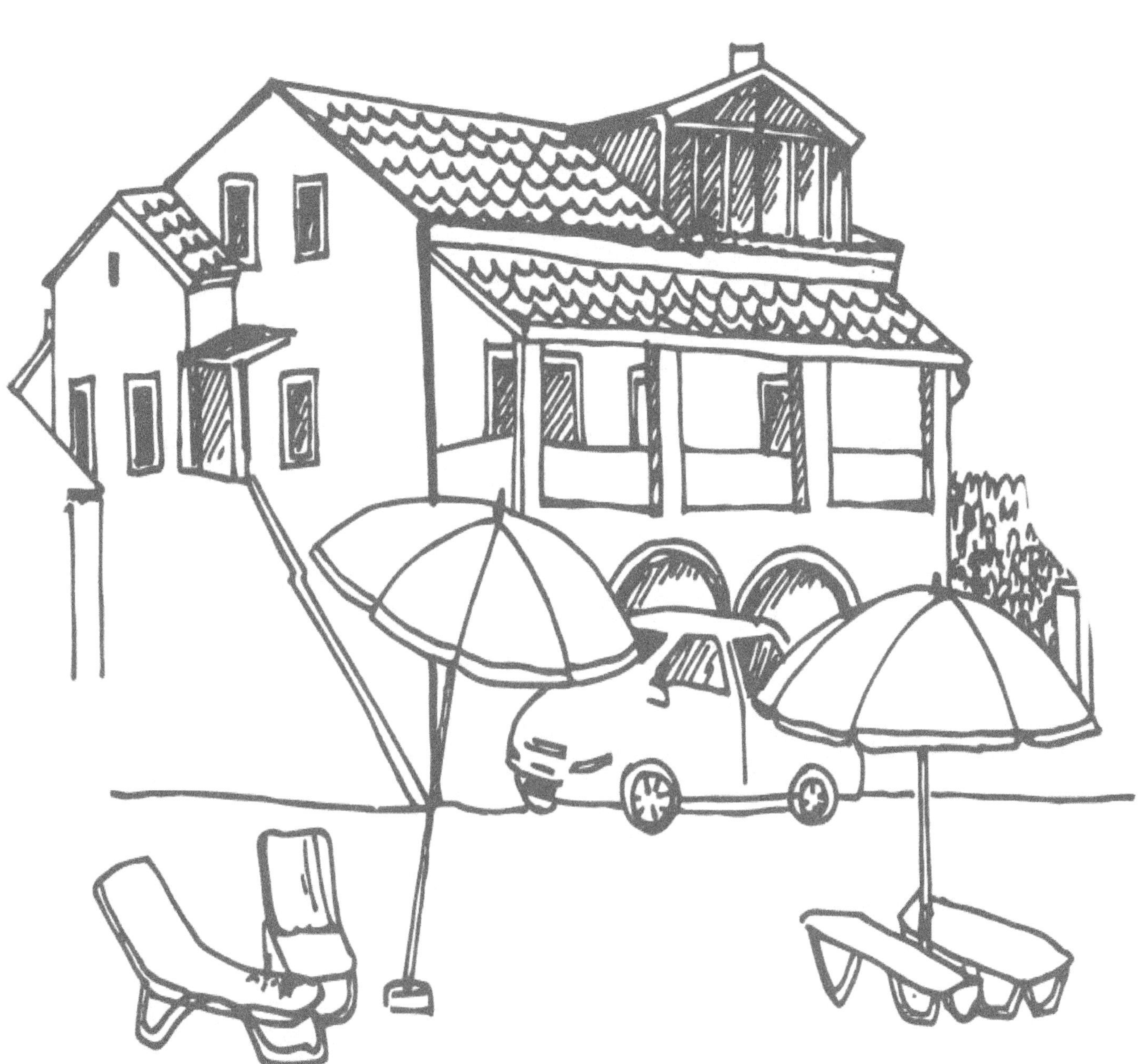

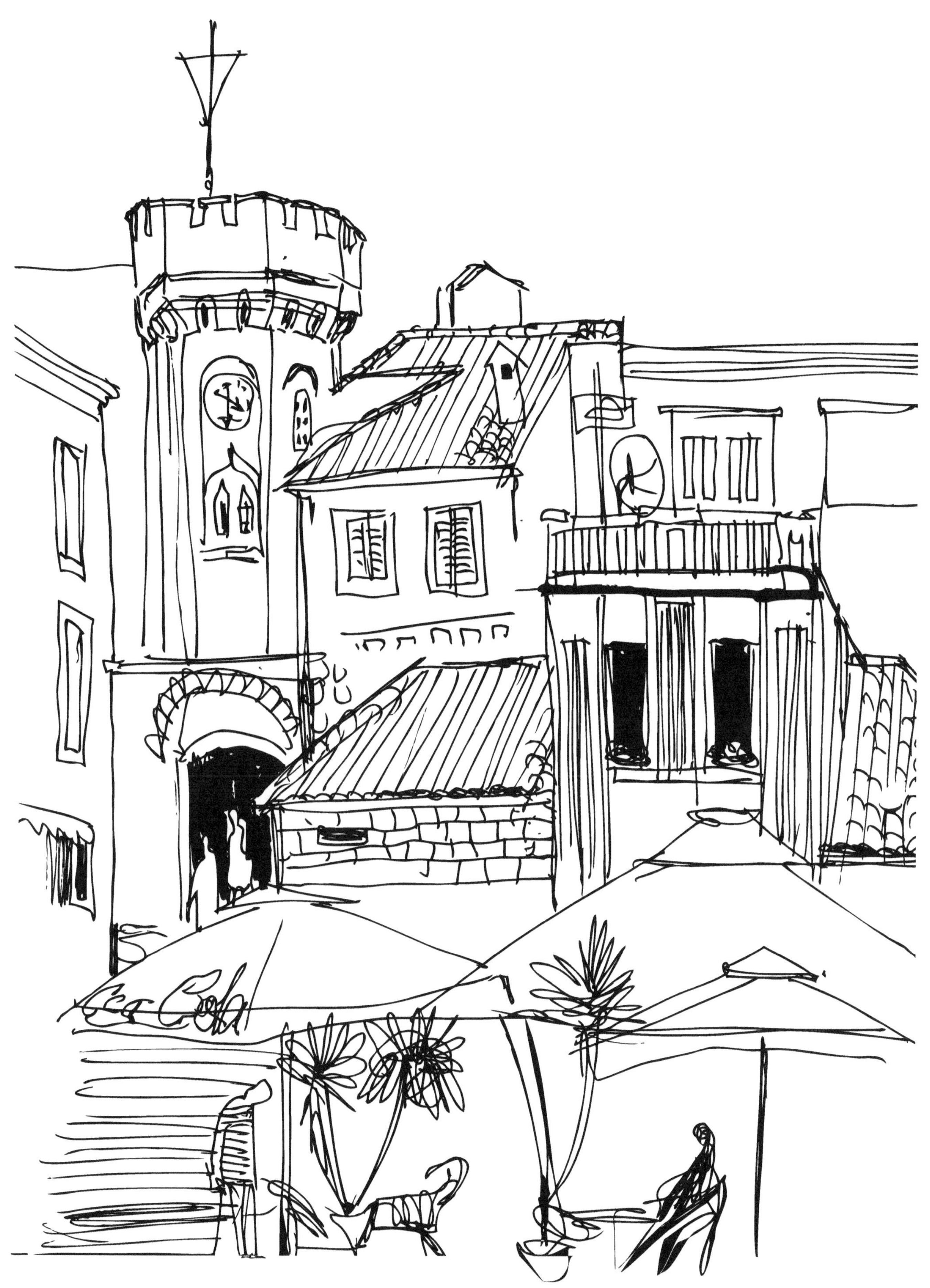

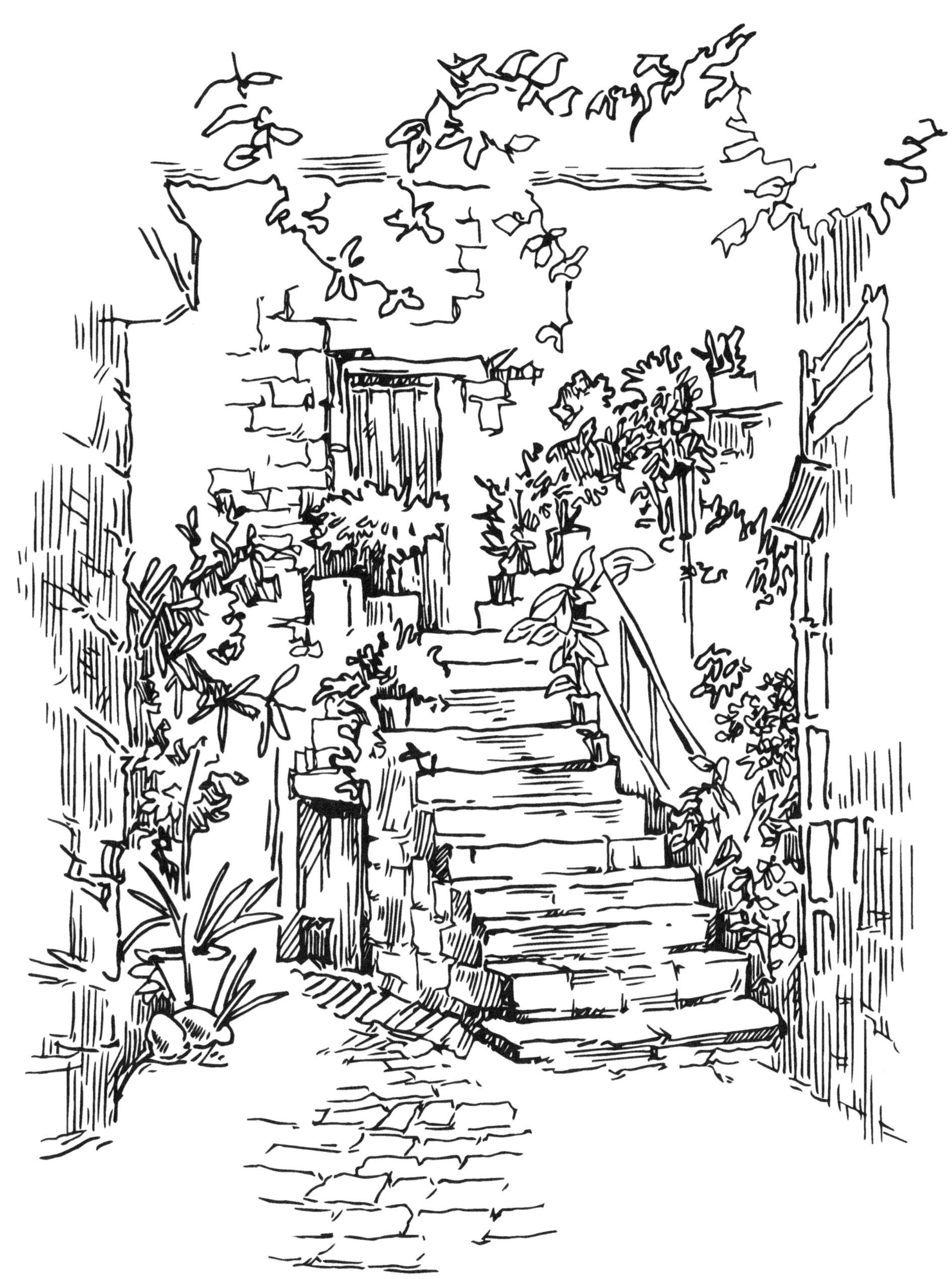

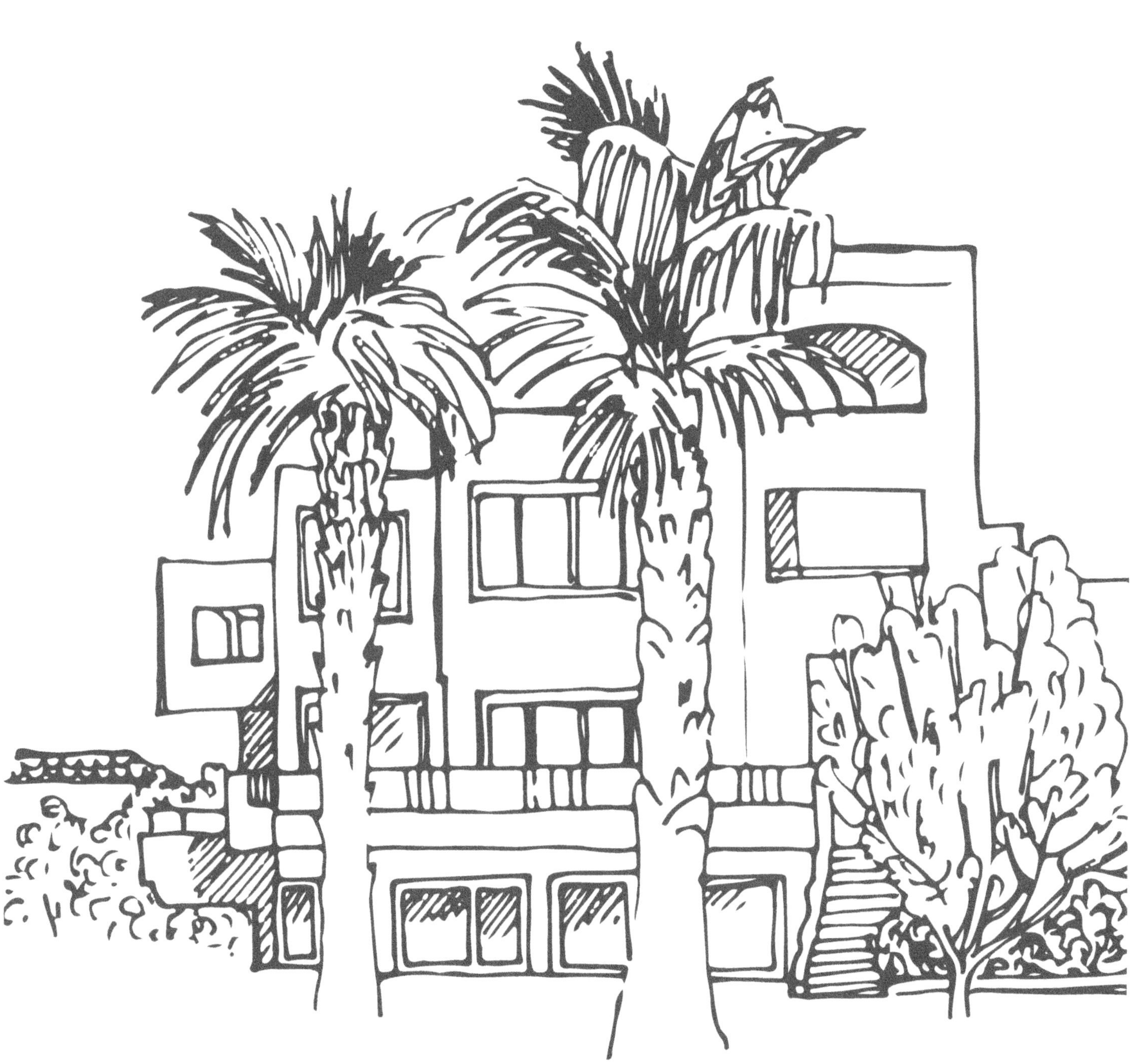

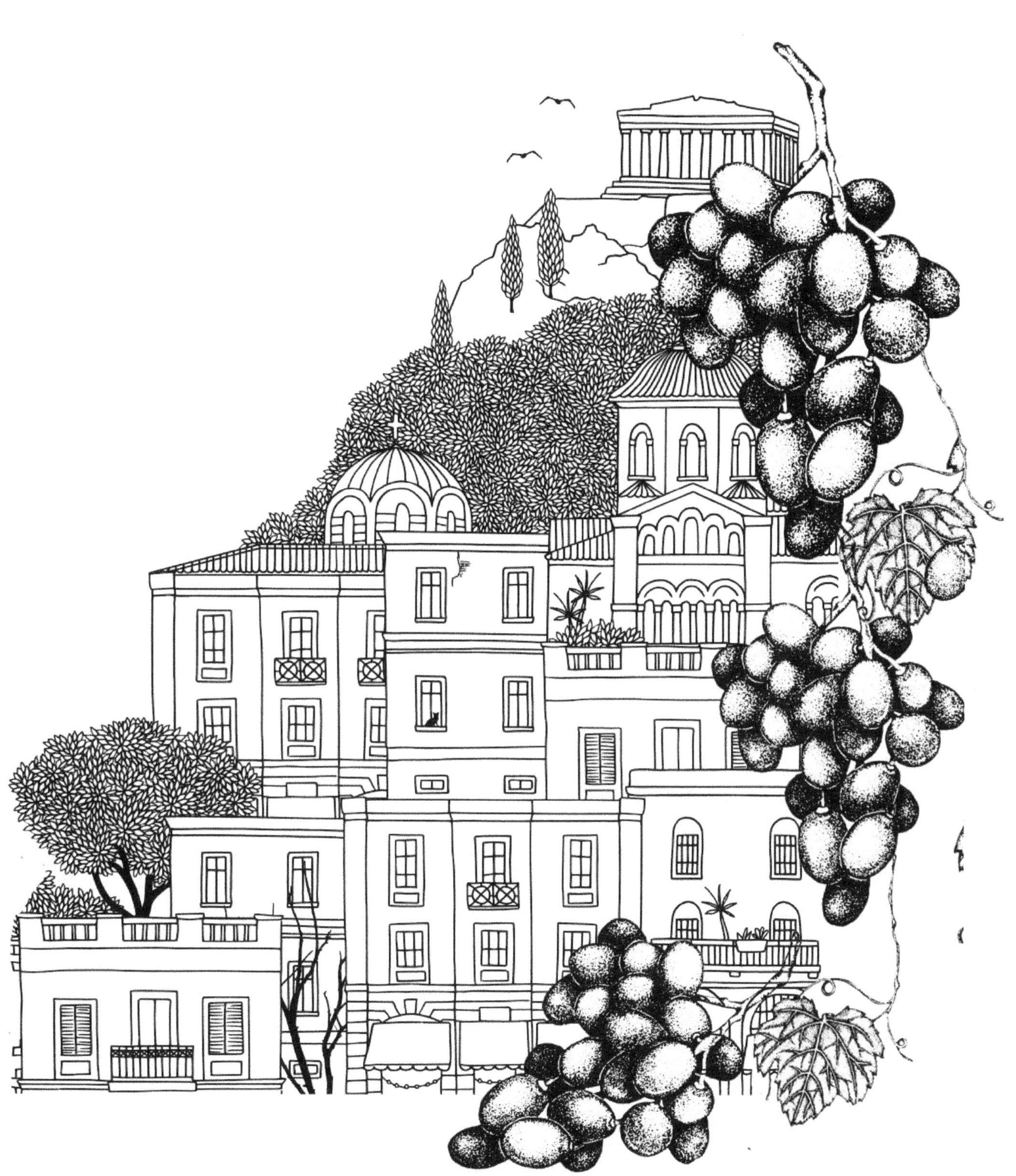

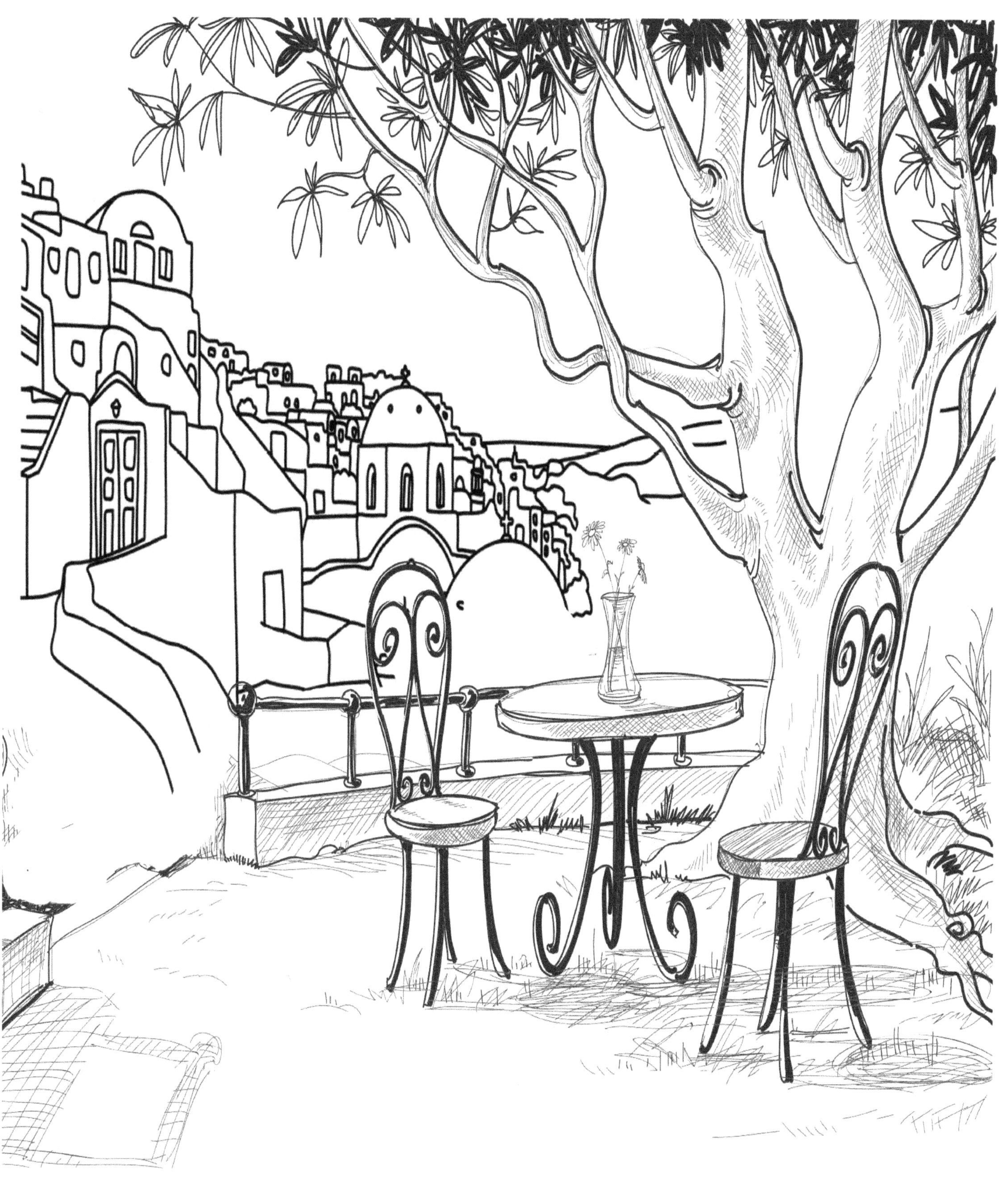

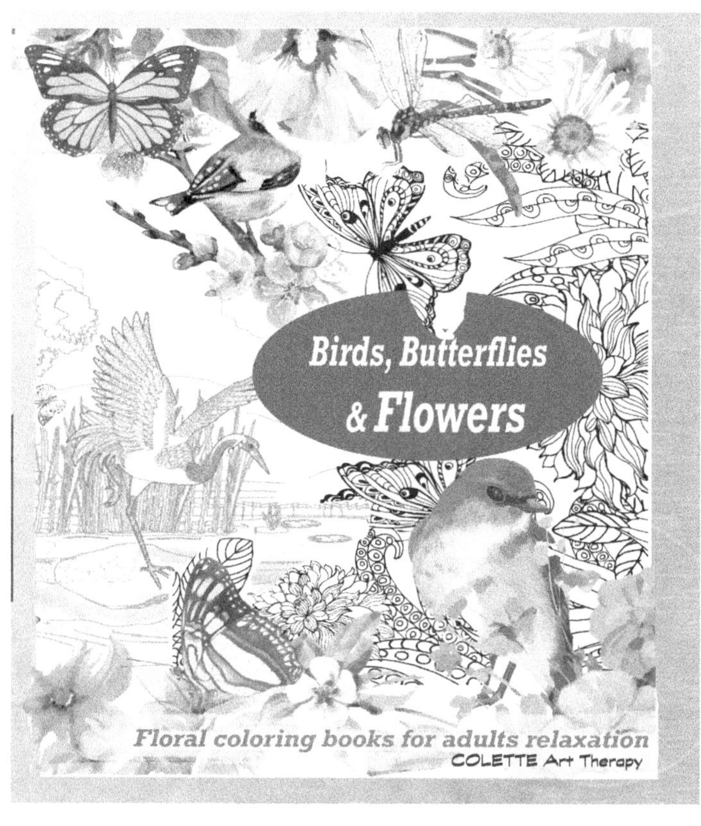

Also available from

Colette Art Therapy:

Birds, Butterflies and Flowers

A coloring Journal of the time during Covid 19 Lockdown.

Adults relaxtion coloring books

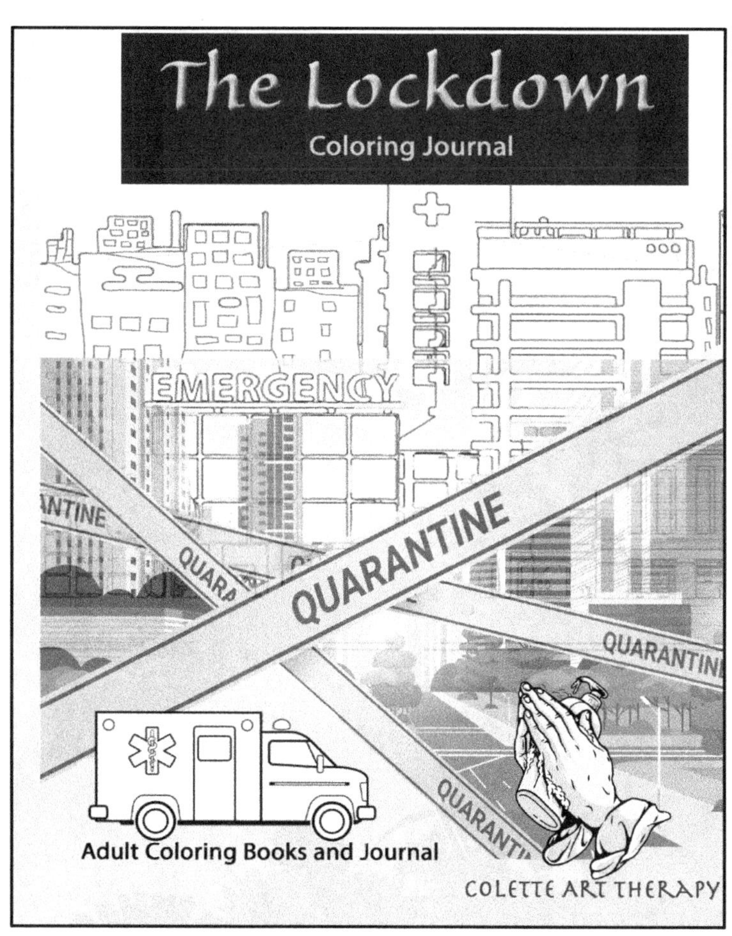

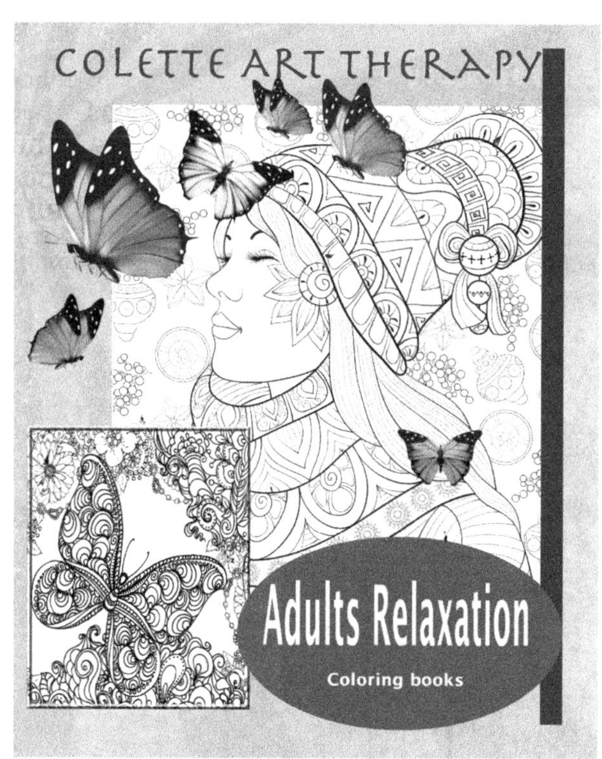

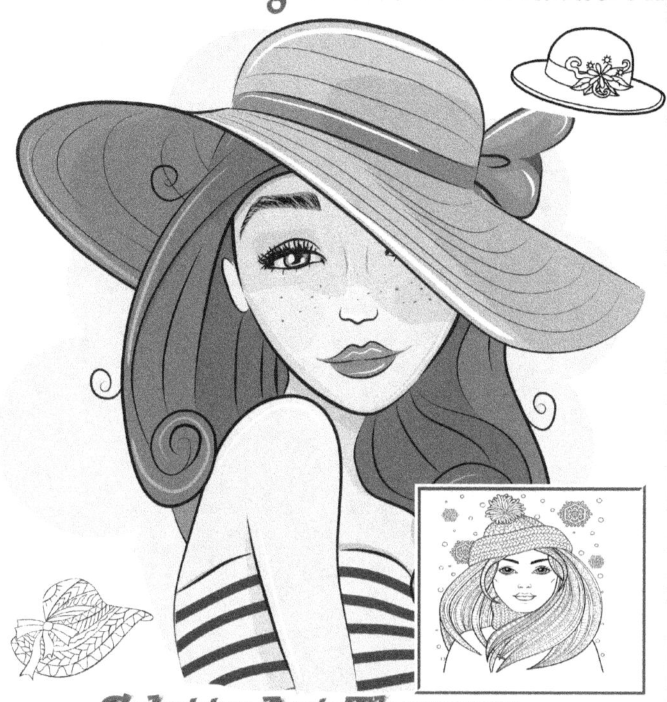

Also available from Colette Art Therapy:

Beautiful
Hats
Design and
Color

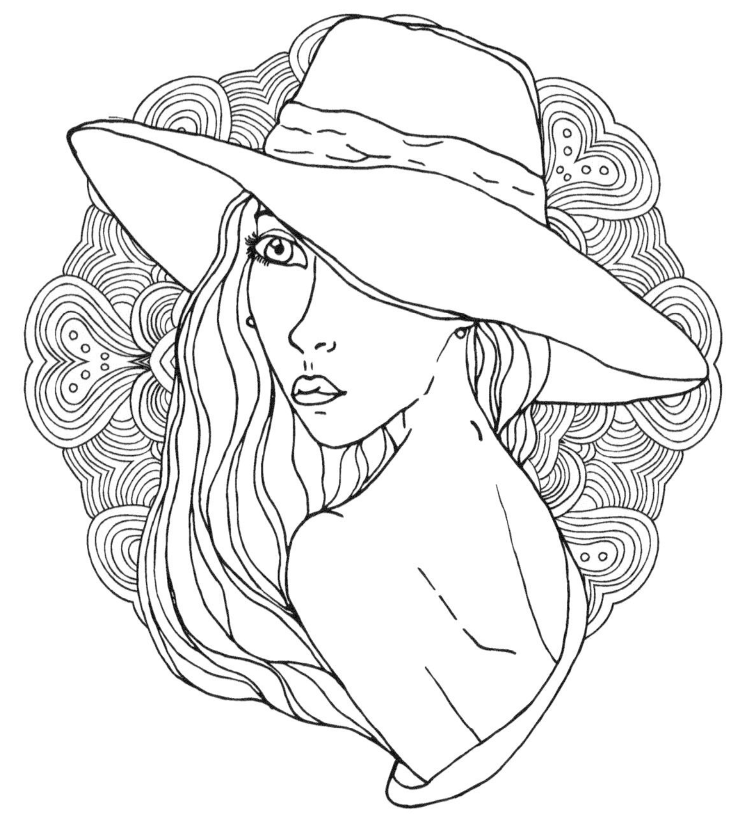

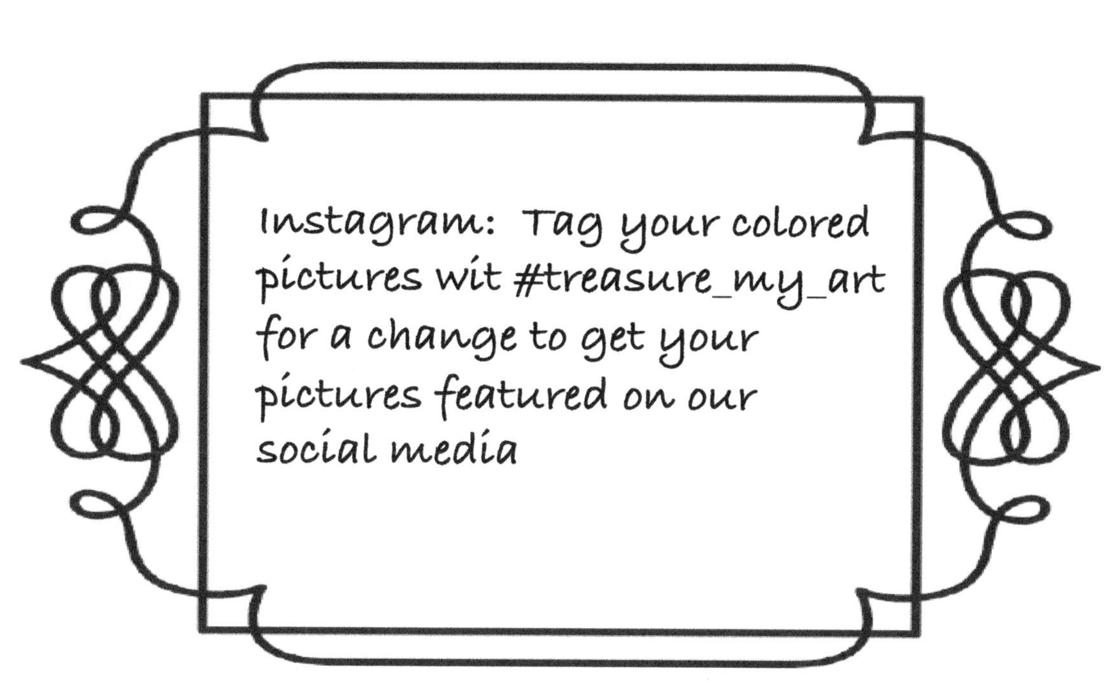

Instagram: Tag your colored pictures wit #treasure_my_art for a change to get your pictures featured on our social media

www.ingramcontent.com/pod-product-compliance
Lightning Source LLC
LaVergne TN
LVHW080612200726
843509LV00007B/294